THE GLORY
AND THE STEAM

THE GLORY AND THE STEAM

The mainly North Eastern diary
of a teenage railway enthusiast
1960-65

John Gilroy

Silver Link Publishing Ltd

First published in 2012

British Library Cataloguing in Publication Data

A catalogue record for this book is available from the British Library.

ISBN 978 1 85794 393 1

Silver Link Publishing Ltd
The Trundle
Ringstead Road
Great Addington
Kettering
Northants NN14 4BW

Tel/Fax: 01536 330588
email: sales@nostalgiacollection.com
Website: www.nostalgiacollection.com

Printed and bound in the Czech Republic

CONTENTS

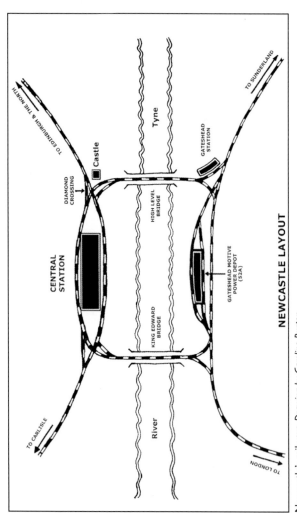

Newcastle's railways. *Drawing by Caroline Burton*

The following labels appear within the diagram:

Tyne

TO EDINBURGH & THE NORTH

TO SUNDERLAND

Castle

GATESHEAD STATION

DIAMOND CROSSING

HIGH LEVEL BRIDGE

CENTRAL STATION

GATESHEAD MOTIVE POWER DEPOT (52A)

NEWCASTLE LAYOUT

KING EDWARD BRIDGE

River

TO CARLISLE

TO LONDON

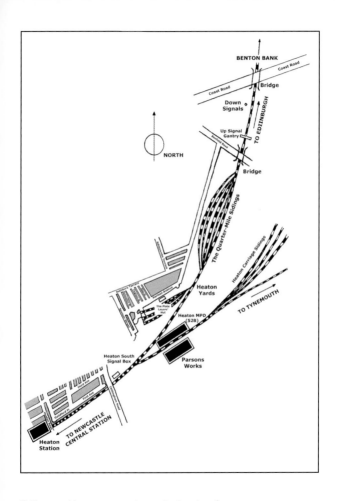

Railways at Heaton – my trainspotting 'territory'.
Drawing by Caroline Burton

ACKNOWLEDGEMENTS

My gratitude is due to Chris Herbert and Emily Burton for their technical support, to Caroline Burton for providing the drawings, and to the Gresley Society for permission to use photographs by the late Dick Orpwood.

INTRODUCTION

When the poet Wordsworth looked back on his earliest days, he spoke of 'something that is gone'. 'Whither is fled the visionary gleam?' he asked. 'Where is it now, the glory and the dream?' In his later years he considered railways a disastrous intrusion on the landscapes that had nurtured his visions. His sonnet 'On the Projected Kendal and Windermere Railway', for example, began, 'Is then no nook of English ground secure / From rash assault?'

By a curious turn of fate, it is the almost 'visionary' memories of those mechanical inventions, deplored by the poet, that now affect many, including me, with much the same sense of Wordsworthian 'loss'. And although he couldn't have anticipated it, even Wordsworth himself might have come to understand. In fact, the analogy is not at all far-fetched. We watchers of steam trains, often unknowingly at the time, were laying up for ourselves memories that only now evoke fully those emotions 'recollected in tranquillity', as Wordsworth describes the sources of his own creativity and poetry.

The wonderful store of impressions from the great days of steam are indeed enduring. Watching as a boy events at Newcastle Central, for example, they would make up for me the grandeur of the Edinburgh-bound express arriving from London, doors flung open, hastening trolleys laden with sacks of post, restaurant cars taking on provisions. Up ahead, the urgent change of engines, steam blasting skywards, and the shouts of bystanders trying to make themselves heard above the din. Then, in no time at all, the whistle, the green flag, and the train on the move again. North of the city and out towards the country, the waving grasses and wild flowers of a lineside in summer, usually a skylark overhead. Between trains, those long pauses when everything seemed to go to sleep. These are abiding sensations in moments that have taken on an indisputable power of the kind that, in the context of his own memories, Wordsworth would refer to as 'spots of time'.

For the title of this volume, therefore, and without the slightest trace of irony, I've adapted the poet's lines to reflect 'The glory and the steam', the recorded observations in my childhood and early teens of 'something that is gone', and which survive as they were preserved in my diary of those times.

Most train-watchers had their favourite locations, but not everyone's personal plot of ground has had the privilege of being recorded in literature. My own 'territory', extending for roughly the 1½ miles between Benton Bank in the north (where the East Coast Main Line begins to climb towards George Stephenson's Killingworth) and, at the southern end, Heaton motive power depot, was famously celebrated in *Kiddar's Luck* (1951) by Jack Common, socialist friend of George Orwell and son of an engine driver at Heaton.

At the beginning of a book that some have called a neglected masterpiece, Common, whom Lawrence Bradshaw took as a model for his bust of Karl Marx in Highgate Cemetery, describes how he 'chose' his origins in my own northern suburb of Newcastle:

KIDDAR'S LUCK

★

Jack Common

★

TURNSTILE PRESS
10 Great Turnstile W.C.1.

'Missing lush Sussex, the Surrey soft spots, affluent Mayfair and gold-filled Golder's Green, fat Norfolk rectories, the Dukeries, and many a solid Yorkshire village, to name only some

The title page of *Kiddar's Luck*.

10

obvious marks, I came upon the frost-rimed roofs of a working-class suburb in Newcastle-upon-Tyne, and in the back-bedroom of an upstairs flat in a street parallel with the railway line, on which a halted engine whistled to be let through the junction, I chose my future parents.'

Between 1903, when Jack Common arrived on the scene, and 1960. when, at the age of 13, I started to keep my diary of train workings in the area, Heaton Junction hadn't changed much. Heaton shed, a subsidiary of Gateshead motive power depot, still hosted a large complement of engines, from humble shunters, freight and mixed-traffic locomotives to the 'Pacific' power of the legendary expresses.

The 'Flying Scotsman', 'Heart of Midlothian', 'Queen of Scots' Pullman, 'North Briton', 'Talisman' and, in

'A3' No 60050 *Persimmon* heads a train for Newcastle Central past Heaton motive power depot (52B) on 14 May 1961. *A. Johns*

The east end of Heaton MPD photographed in 1970 after it had officially closed. The track on the left serviced the C.A. Parsons engineering works.

'A3' No 60112 *St Simon* reverses at Heaton MPD on 27 March 1960.
A. Johns

A diesel unit passes the south end of the closed Heaton MPD in July 1970.

summertime, the 'Elizabethan', non-stop from King's Cross to Edinburgh, would come storming through Heaton station to take the long curve north through the junction and past Heaton marshalling yards towards Berwick, Edinburgh and beyond.

Every observation point had its advantages. At First Avenue, where the track ran parallel with the Victorian terraced streets of the suburb, the great expresses could be watched from above, through iron railings and the leaves of lineside trees.

How huge and powerful those engines were as they came

'A1' No 60159 *Bonnie Dundee* passes First Avenue, Heaton, on the northbound 'Flying Scotsman' on 3 July 1959. *A. Johns*

'A2' No 60521 *Watling Street* approaches Newcastle at First Avenue, also heading the 'Flying Scotsman', on 17 July 1959. *A. Johns*

'A4' No 60017 *Silver Fox* travels light to Heaton MPD past First Avenue after bringing in the 'Talisman' from King's Cross. *A. Johns*

'B16/2' No 61435 takes a northbound tank wagon train past First Avenue on 17 July 1959. *A. Johns*

At the same spot 'A4' No 60004 *William Whitelaw* succeeds No 60017 on the Newcastle–Waverley section of the 'Talisman'. *A. Johns*

17

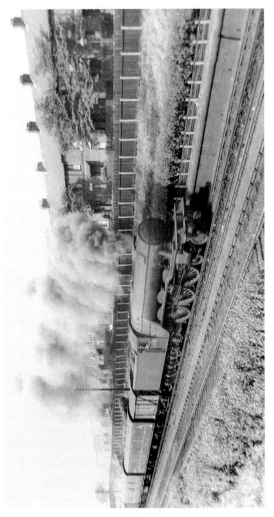

Finally in this sequence, 'A3' No 60038 *Firdaussi* heads the northbound 11.53am ex-Newcastle Royal Mail train on 17 July 1959. *A. Johns*

through, trembling the ground and leaving behind a smoky, slightly sweetish, haze as their mark of passage. To me, as an uninformed child, their names were often incongruous – *Tranquil*, *Pretty Polly* – or challenging – *Isinglass*, *Sayajirao*. I would learn, of course, that these were, among many others, the names of classic racehorses, just as on first reading the novels of Walter Scott I learned the source of names, to me much more familiar on locomotives, such as *Meg Merrilies*, *Guy Mannering*, *Madge Wildfire*, *Hal o'the Wynd*.

There was something entirely appropriate about this. North of Newcastle, the line to Scotland makes its way through Northumberland and Scott's own Border country. Jack Common describes the 'coastal track':

'Amble, Warkworth, Alnmouth, Alnwick, Seahouses, Bamborough, Christon Bank, Belford, Beale (for Holy Island), Tweedmouth, Berwick. Everywhere the railway lines ran they were bound to meet castles, battlefields and holy places [...]. Lucky man, my father, to be paid to puff his way in a local invention across the very tables of chronicle and story, his cab-window an eye scanning the centuries every day.'

Such memorable mixtures of history and romance, as well as of local engineering achievements, lent to the railways with which I was familiar a particular atmosphere that will never come again. Adjacent to Heaton sheds was Parsons works, named for Sir Charles Parsons, inventor of the steam turbine. To have been born in Newcastle at that time and brought up in the suburb of Heaton was almost to have steam in the blood. All day and late into the evening freight trains for the north departed from the sidings known as 'The Quarter-Mile', guards waving an 'all-clear' lamp to their distant drivers as they headed towards Scotland and the Borders.

At night in bed I would know what time it was from the chime whistle of an 'A4' 'Pacific' as it went south through Heaton Junction with the 'Night Scotsman' or the

Rothbury Terrace, Heaton: what were known as 'The Quarter-Mile' sidings are seen here looking south towards the C.A. Parsons engineering works in July 1970. The East Coast Main Line, north and south, is immediately in front of the lineside hut.

'Aberdonian'. Each day brought its endlessly changing, ever-interesting, sequence of train workings from dawn until dark.

The great 'Pacific' locomotives of those days were familiar to 'spotters' along the whole length of the East Coast line. Their names made them distinct as individuals, and when one appeared at the head of a freight, quietly awaiting the right of way in the 'Quarter-Mile' sidings for an hour or so on a summer evening, or stood light engine alongside the platelayers' hut, it made possible a personal encounter with a national celebrity. The locomotive might be a 'namer', which until now had proved elusive. 'Spotters' took their acquisition of named engines very seriously and, for all of us, some of those engines would be destined to remain forever unobtainable. The innocent pencillings on lineside properties or station columns, which were all that passed for graffiti in those days, told their 'tragic' tales: 'I died here waiting for Sun Castle ... or Earl Marischal.' 'I died here waiting for Wolf of Badenoch...' I doubt whether the same is being written of power cars called *Bromley Travelwise*, *London Borough of Havering Celebrating 40 Years*, or even *Fairbridge – Investing in the Future*.

One of my earliest memories as a small boy is arriving

The platelayers' hut, Marleen Avenue, Heaton Junction, July 1970 – a favourite 'spotting' vantage point.

at Newcastle Central and an aunt, on my behalf, asking the driver of our train what the locomotive's name was. In his soft Geordie lilt he replied, 'Oh, it hasn't got a name, pet. But mine's Monty, if that'll do.'

Today, trains such as the 'Trans-Siberian' or 'Orient Express', preserving the albeit manufactured vestiges of a bygone age, are the commonly recognised properties of travel literature or crime fiction. But that routine and personal engagement with the world of romance and imagination, once part of the everyday working scene on the steam railways of the British Isles is, sadly, no more a possibility.

The following pages, therefore, tell a story. They record, first of all, the rapid demise of a complex, labour-intensive system dating back to the Victorian era that was still largely in place at the beginning of the 1960s. The first entry in this account of my observations is in February 1960, when I was 13 years old, the last in 1965. In little more than five years, what had seemed to be forever features of the entire British landscape, the steam locomotive and all the familiar and time-honoured paraphernalia that accompanied it, would have simply dwindled away with hardly a trace remaining. Second, this is the naïve account of a child who, when he started to write it, had no idea that one day he would be offering it up to public scrutiny. So the slow development in style, from that of schoolboy to young adult, now probably of interest only to its author, is a kind of sub-text to the primary story it tells. To preserve the integrity of the document, the presentation in its original form has been preserved. Only the slightest amendments have been made for the purposes of clarification, with some running commentary here and there on the observations detailed, and a few further reflections, from the perspective of now almost half a century, appearing in square brackets.

MY DIARY

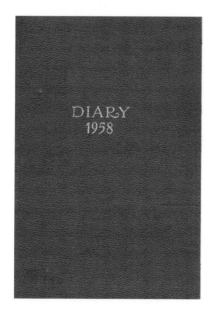

My railway diary.

Age 13
1960

[I was also keeping a daily personal diary at this time and some of its remarks, where they coincide with my railway diary observations, appear here and there. The entry for 27 February 1960, reads: 'Been trainspotting all day. Saw lots of these new big diesel engines.'

Unless specifically identified as being located elsewhere, all entries below refer to lineside observations in the Heaton area of Newcastle-upon-Tyne.]

Saturday 27 February 1960

'A4' No 60012 *Commonwealth of Australia* heads north with a passenger train at 10.00am.

See it again going north with a King's Cross-Glasgow train at 4.25pm.

'A3' No 60093 *Coronach* leaves Heaton Yards with a northbound freight during the morning.

At 2.50pm D239 heads south through Heaton Junction.

'B1' No 61032 *Stembok* is a light engine at Benfield Road.

Here is my complete list of numbers: 60093, 63363, 63434, 90072, D245, 60012, 64704, 64938, D237, 61032, 60913, 92175, D239, 65804, D245.

[In this, the first of my recorded observations, it is clear that the diesel age has dawned.]

Sunday 28 February 1960

Saw diesel engine D245 hurtling northwards through Heaton with a goods train.

[Diary entry: 'At night watched Bruce Forsyth at the London Palladium on ITV.']

Monday 29 February 1960

Today I saw 'A4' No 60028 *Walter K. Whigham* as light engine at Benfield Road. Then it moved away and I didn't see it again.. Then I saw 'A3' No 60083 *Sir Hugo* moving out of Heaton Yards with a northbound goods. I saw 'A3' No 60058 *Blair Athol* rushing southwards, as also 'A1' No 60116 *Hal o'the Wynd* with the 'Queen of Scots' Pullman about 20 minutes later. Moving at about 40mph through Heaton Junction was 'A3' No 60085 *Manna* whose once bright green livery has been reduced to a dirty grey.

Here is the list of numbers: 60028, 60085, 64864, 63352, 60058, 60116, 64923, 63394, 60083, 61854, 68732, 65797.

[Diary entry: 'Watched Charlie Drake, *Double Your Money* and *The Larkins* on TV.']

'A3' No 60083 *Sir Hugo* at First Avenue, Heaton, with a northbound goods. *R. F. Orpwood, the Gresley Society*

Saturday 12 March 1960

[Diary entry: 'Bought new locospotter's book – great! Found good new place to trainspot, at the bottom of Spencer Street. At night watched ITV film *The Years Between*.]

This morning I saw 'V2' No 60883 in Heaton Junction. Also 'V2' No 60860 *Durham School* was standing by the platelayers' hut. Diesel D247 was seen speeding through the junction with a southbound Pullman. It gave two clear musical notes and one dull grating note on its horn. 'A4' No 60006 *Sir Ralph Wedgwood* left Heaton Carriage Sidings

No 60085 *Manna* with 'A3' No 60036 *Colombo* (left) and 'A4' No 60019 *Bittern* (right) at Gateshead MPD (52A) on 15 September 1963.
R. F. Orpwood, the Gresley Society

Heaton Carriage Sidings looking east in July 1970.

with a train of empty coaches for Newcastle Central. At about 1.55pm 'A1' No 60147 *North Eastern* came through the junction with a southbound passenger train. The northbound 'Flying Scotsman' had 'A1' No 60115 *Meg Merrilies*.

Another interesting item I saw today was a goods brake van being made ready for use. This I saw at Spencer Street sidings (over the fence). First of all the cleaner opened the door of the van. He then tipped out the ash from the fire. After this he placed the lamps on the back and lit them. Then he extinguished them. Finally, he got down and chalked the destination on the side.

Here is the list of numbers: 60115, 60887, 62041, 67658, 60147, D247, 64856, 60006, 60934, 65804, 60860, 60883, 65831.

Spencer Street sidings, Heaton Junction, looking towards Heaton MPD and Parsons engineering works.

Saturday 19 March 1960

The first train I saw today was the 'North Briton' headed by a bright green diesel D238. It crawled past Benfield Road and headed away towards Glasgow.

Then 'A2' No 60510 *Robert the Bruce* pulled out of the Quarter-Mile heading northwards with a heavy goods train. It took a short while for it to get moving and the weight of the train kept making its driving wheels slip. However, it soon accelerated and was going quite quickly when its guards van passed me. 'K3' No 61952 also came and stood by itself.

A short goods train headed southwards by 'J72' No 68738 stopped under the signal gantry at Benfield Road. Afterwards I saw this engine from my post in Spencer Street with the same train. Whilst standing at this spot I noticed the double arm signal was up so I raced down to Marleen Avenue on my bicycle and was just in time to see diesel D245 moving southwards with the King's Cross-bound 'Flying Scotsman'. It gave only one high-pitched sound on its horn as it passed through Heaton. About five minutes later the signal for the south was up again. However, a two-coach diesel car train was all that came through. It gave a much more powerful blast on its horn.

Today I also saw a southbound Pullman headed by D237. 'A1' No 60142 *Edward Fletcher* headed the northward-bound 'Flying Scotsman'. 'A4' No 60009 *Union of South Africa* hurtled through the junction heading south with the 'Heart of Midlothian'. A handsome engine 'V2' No 60825 pulled a long freight train northwards. I raced it along the Quarter-Mile on my bicycle, but it gradually overtook me. 9F No 92036 and 'K3' No 61930 headed north coupled together.

[Diary entry: 'Watched *Dodge City*, a film about cowboys, and the serial *Samuel Pepys*.]

I took it along the ½ mile and then it
slowly moved away from me.
Then no. 42016 and 61630 backed North
coupled together.

21-3-60 . Central Station (Newcastle - on - Tyne)

On platform 8 . at about 1.15 pm 'The
Talisman pulled in headed by no 60009
A.4. Union of South Africa'. It was headed
north. It stood about 5 minutes and then
slowly pulled out again. Once the first
few pulls from these engines are over, the
train soon begins to accelerate. The next
A.4 engine was no. 60001 'Sir Ronald
Matthews' looking equally as powerful. It
made a deafening noise as it pulled its
train in. Then no. 60081 'Shotover' took
over the train and headed north.
            Another A.4 streamlined
engine no. 60024 'Kingfisher' brought in
a train Southwards.

No. 60083 'Sir Hugo' pulled an empty
train straight through Northwards, on
platform 9.
        Then about 10 minutes later
A.3 class. no. 60064. Tagalie. hauled a
Northward bound train into platform 8.
Then it uncoupled and went off, in the
direction of Gateshead sheds.
        Almost as soon as it
had gone A.4 no. 60011 'Empire of India'
thundered into platform 9 heading South
wards.
        Later over the footbridge we
were just in time to see A.1 class no.
60127. William Wordsell' bring the Queen
of Scots pullman into platform 4. headed
of Southwards. It uncoupled however and
no. 60036 'Colombo' backed gently on
and coupled up. Inside the pullman I
could see the chefs and waiters walking
up and down the train. All the doors
were open and the general hubbub was

On Platform 8 at about 1.15pm the 'Talisman' pulled
in headed by 'A4' No 60009 *Union of South Africa*. It was
headed north. It stood for about 5 minutes and then slowly
pulled out again. Once the first few pulls from these engines
are over, the train soon begins to accelerate. The next engine
to arrive was 'A4' No 60001 *Sir Ronald Matthews* looking
equally as powerful. It made a deafening noise as it pulled its
train in. Then 'A3' No 60081 *Shotover* took over the train
and headed north.

Another streamlined engine 'A4' No 60024 *Kingfisher*
brought in a train southwards.

'A3' No 60083 *Sir Hugo* pulled an empty train straight
through northwards on Platform 9. Then about 10 minutes
later 'A3' No 60064 *Tagalie* headed a northward-bound
train into Platform 8. Then it uncoupled and went off in the
direction of Gateshead Sheds.

'A4' No 60001 *Sir Ronald Matthews* at its home shed, Gateshead (52A), on 2 May 1964. *R. F. Orpwood, the Gresley Society*

'A3' 60064 *Tagalie* gets ready to depart from Platform 9 at Newcastle Central with the southbound 'Heart of Midlothian' on 21 March 1960.

Almost as soon as it had gone 'A4' No 60011 *Empire of India* thundered into Platform 9 heading southwards. Its fireman gave me a wave.

Later, over the footbridge, we were just in time to see 'A1' Class No 60127 *Wilson Worsdell* bring the 'Queen of Scots' Pullman into Platform 9 headed southwards. It uncoupled and 'A3' No 60036 *Colombo* backed gently on and coupled up. Inside the Pullman I could see the chefs and waiters walking up and down the train. All the doors were open and a general hubbub was going on. Meanwhile *Colombo* was making a deafening noise, oil and water poured from it and it looked in grand condition. Then finally it moved out, its big driving wheels slipping and sending showers of sparks into the air.

Then a diesel-electric engine D247 took over a short passenger train heading southwards. It accelerated extraordinarily quickly, making palls of dense blue fumes as it went (I saw this engine on 12.3.60 with a King's Cross Pullman).

'A1' No 60127 *Wilson Worsdell* at Heaton MPD on 12 May 1962.
R. F. Orpwood, the Gresley Society

Running over to the other platform (No 8), I was just in time to see the northward-bound 'Flying Scotsman' headed by 'A4' No 60013 *Dominion of New Zealand*. This engine soon uncoupled and 'A4' No 60016 *Silver King* coupled up. This is a very powerful-looking engine. I could see its white-hot fire and all its controls. It gave its low treble-noted whistle and slowly thundered out. I managed to photograph

'A4' No 60016 *Silver King* awaits departure on the northbound 'Flying Scotsman' at Newcastle Central on 21 March 1960.

it. Going back to Platform 9 I saw 'A3' No 60096 *Papyrus* bring in a train southwards. I succeeded in photographing it and also its successor 'A3' No 60064 *Tagalie*. This engine I had seen earlier, and it now took over the train, the 'Heart of Midlothian'. It was then that I saw a special type of engine, No 92061 (fitted with air pumps to operate Tyne Dock mineral trains). Another diesel-electric passed by on its own behind the station.

'A1' No 60524 *Herringbone* took out a goods train on another platform.

'A3' No 60096 *Papyrus* arrives at Newcastle from Edinburgh on the 'Heart of Midlothian', also on 21 March 1960.

'A4' No 60024 *Kingfisher* backs onto an Edinburgh-bound express at Newcastle Central on the afternoon of 21 March 1960.

Finally 'A1' No 60147 *North Eastern* brought a train into Platform 8 northwards. I photographed it. Then 'A4' No 60024 *Kingfisher* took over again. I had also seen this engine earlier. On leaving the station I saw diesel D257. I could not photograph it as I had run out of film. Quite a busy day in fact.

[Diary entry: 'Been off school for St Cuthbert's Day. In the afternoon, went to the Central trainspotting with Michael Watson. Saw six streamlined engines among which was *Silver King*.' Each year in honour of St Cuthbert we were given a day's holiday from our toils at St Cuthbert's Grammar School (my alma mater, as well as that of Sting, the pop singer, Dec, of Ant and Dec fame, and Neil Tennant of the Pet Shop Boys). I particularly mention *Silver King*, whose name was, and I suspect still is, for my generation, inseparable from its association with Hornby's model version of the 'A4' locomotive, an important item in many a boy's electric train set at the time, including my own.]

Saturday 23 April 1960

I saw a number of interesting engines and also a lot of interesting activities today. 'V2s' Nos 60951, 60835, 60816, 'A4' No 60009 *Union of South Africa* heading north. Having recently obtained Ian Allan's book *British Express Trains* I am able to see the trains at their scheduled times, and speeds, distances are included. 'B1' No 61018 *Gnu*, an engine I had not seen before, went into the junction at Heaton. I also timed the northbound 'Flying Scotsman' headed by diesel-electric D239.

[Diary entry: 'Most likely going to see Cliff Richard at Newcastle City Hall on May 4th. Went trainspotting. All trains came through exactly as the book said.' The reference is to Cecil J. Allen, *British Express Trains, No 5 Anglo-Scottish services and Scottish Region*, 2/6d. The 'B1' *Gnu* carried, I think, the shortest nameplate of all named locomotives. My hopes as a 13-year-old in 1960 of seeing Cliff Richard were not finally realised until 50 years later when, at the age of 63, I did eventually see him (with the Shadows) at the O2 London on 28 September 2009!]

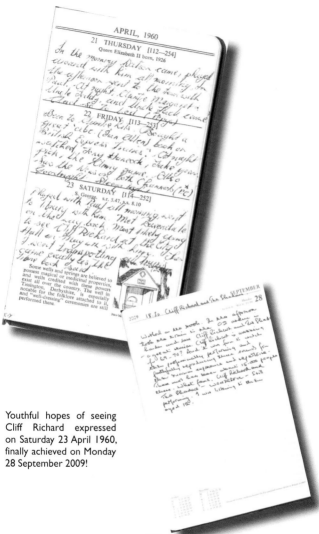

Youthful hopes of seeing Cliff Richard expressed on Saturday 23 April 1960, finally achieved on Monday 28 September 2009!

Age 14
1960-61

Wednesday 15 June 1960
[Diary entry: 'In the morning bought the Everly Brothers' record *Cathy's Clown* which is number one at the moment. Went trainspotting.' Here, regrettably, my personal diary entries for 1960 cease.]

Engines seen: 'A3' No 60099 *Call Boy*, 'A1' No 60162 *Saint Johnstoun*. Diesels Nos D249, D246, D256, D270, D238, 'V2s' 60892, 60940, 65819, 63378, 77011, 61934.

Wednesday 10 August 1960
Concentrating on large 'Pacifics' mostly today. 'A4' No 60019 *Bittern* headed north with an un-named train. Later in the afternoon I saw the 'Elizabethan' heading north pulled by 'A4' No 60032 *Gannet*.

This 'A4' 'Pacific' is allocated to King's Cross shed and was through Newcastle only because the 'Elizabethan' is non-stop. Also saw Gresley 'A3' 'Pacific' No 60074

'A4' No 60032 *Gannet*. R. F. Orpwood, the Gresley Society

40

Harvester and 'A1' 'Pacific' Thompson design No 60126 *Sir Vincent Raven*.

Thursday 11 August 1960
11.20am: Gresley 'A4' 'Pacific' No 60005 *Sir Charles Newton* headed north with an un-named train. 11.45am: Gresley 'A4' 'Pacific' 60032 *Gannet*, which I saw yesterday, was returning south with the 'Elizabethan'.

Diesels 1-Co-Co-1 Type 4 English Electric Nos D247, D257, D244, D270, D271.

In the afternoon I saw Gresley 'A4' 'Pacific' No 60016 *Silver King* returning home light engine.

Monday 22 August 1960
Engines seen: 'A3' No 60100 *Spearmint*, 'A3' No 60043 *Brown Jack*, 'A2' No 60539 *Bronzino*, D243, D242, 'V2' 60925.

Tuesday 23 August 1960
Engines seen: 'A4' No 60027 *Merlin*, 'A1' No 60127 *Wilson Worsdell*.

Description of rail journey Newcastle-Carlisle in the summer of 1960
[This little narrative, offered here in its 'unimproved' state, was probably composed as a way of pre-empting the time-honoured school essay requirement, 'What I did in my summer holidays'.]

Towards the close of these summer holidays I was fortunate enough to make a journey by rail and road around the English Lakes. The train (a diesel railcar) left Newcastle at 9.08am. After quickly accelerating it moved through the jumble of lines leading to Scotswood Road. I noticed a small 0-6-0 tank engine painted a bright SR green [actually NE] with a brass steam dome, which was shunting near the station [a reference to one of the two celebrated 'J72' station

'J72s' Nos 68736 and 68723 in NE green livery at Gateshead MPD on 18 September 1963. *R. F. Orpwood, the Gresley Society*

pilots at Newcastle Central, Nos 68736 and 68723, which, in addition to the British Railways logo, also carried the pre-grouping NER crest].

We soon travelled along at a rate of about 40mph along the narrow railway beside Scotswood Road where the train almost literally scrapes the walls of Vickers-Armstrong's works. [The specific references to speeds suggest that I had found a seat behind the driver and could see the speedometer.]

We soon entered good scenery. Running parallel with the Tyne we passed through Elswick station, then through Blaydon and Prudhoe. Our train then began to slow and kept up a pace of about 18mph. It is a very bad part of the line and trains must always take it slowly [whether this was true or not I have no idea].

However, we soon picked up speed again and our train quickly passed Riding Mill. We touched 60mph near Corbridge and I noticed 'A1' No 60115 *Meg Merrilies* flash past in the other direction with a long freight train. Then our train sounded its horn and ground to a stop at Hexham. Three minutes later we started again through Haydon Bridge, Bardon Mill and Henshaw at a leisurely pace of about 45mph. The diesel sounded its horn again and stopped at Haltwhistle (a very appropriate name). Our next station which we passed through was Brampton Junction. Then we slowed to about 20mph through Kingmoor where I saw No 45729 *Furious*. Then we pulled into Carlisle station where No 72005 *Clan Macgregor* was seen coupled to another engine. Other locomotives seen during the day were Nos 45738 *Samson*, No 46230 *Duchess of Buccleuch*, 'V2' No 60804, No 45642 *Boscawen*.

[Hedging my bets, the following was written up also, I suspect, with an eye to the first English composition of the Autumn term. Its incompletion suggests that I'd decided after all that the previous one would probably fit the bill.]

Highlight train journey of 1960 described

On July 31 1960, having spent an enjoyable week's holiday in Edinburgh, we made our way to Waverley station for the return journey home. Our train was 'The Flying Scotsman', due to leave Edinburgh at 10.00am and reach Newcastle at 12.15pm.

At 10.00am precisely it moved out, headed by a Type 4 1-Co-Co-1 diesel No D252, which sounded a departing blast on its horn. We quickly pulled away from the station and immediately entered the long tunnel leading from Waverley.

Once out of the tunnel we accelerated past St Margaret's locomotive depot with its scores of diesel shunters and old steam engines. We passed Portobello station at about 45mph, and just as the speed had climbed to about 60mph the grating sound of the brakes was heard and we came to a halt near Drem. It began to rain. In the quietness I could hear D252's engines making that whispering-whining sound so characteristic of diesels. [This was a prescient remark as the Type 4 diesels came to be known to trainspotters as 'Whistlers'.]

For about 20 minutes we were stopped, until a passenger train for Edinburgh came the other way. Then we started. Our diesel would have to make up a lot of time, and it did. We passed Drem, East Linton at a steady 75mph. Through Dunbar we raced, occasionally passing a down passenger train.' [Here the narrative breaks off to be followed by a few reflections.]

Gresley A4s have worked quite a lot in the summer. The 'Elizabethan' was hauled through July, August and September by Nos 60027 *Merlin* and 60032 *Gannet*. In September No 60025 *Falcon* took over from Gannet. The 'Talisman' has been hauled mostly by 'A3s', Nos 60089 *Felstead*, 60043 *Brown Jack*, 60042 *Singapore*. Type 4 English Electric diesels have been very common. I had a look round one of them in the Central, D286.

[Excitingly, the driver of D286 had taken a group of us

'spotters' into the cab and through the engine room one afternoon as it waited to depart south from Platform 10 at Newcastle Central station. He became rather irritated with us when, in the middle of his explanations, we all pressed

'A4' No 60027 *Merlin. R. F. Orpwood, the Gresley Society*

One of the plaques carried by No 60027, presented by the Admiralty shore base HMS *Merlin. R. F. Orpwood, the Gresley Society*

'A1' No 60129 *Guy Mannering* at Gateshead MPD on 18 September 1963. *R. F. Orpwood, the Gresley Society*

our noses to the portholes of the engine room to 'spot' a 'Pacific'-hauled express arriving on an adjacent platform.]

Saturday 22 October 1960

'V2' No 60952 passed north in the morning heading a goods train. Returning home light was 'A4' No 60019 *Bittern*, as also were 'A1s' Nos 60135 *Madge Wildfire* and 60129 *Guy Mannering*.

At Benfield Road 'A2' No 60538 *Velocity* moved up the north line, light engine. It was followed by 'A4' No 60024 *Kingfisher* heading a goods train north. At 11.40am the 'North Briton' passed north headed by Type 4 diesel-electric D286. I have been on this same engine at Newcastle Central [see previous entry]. Another Type 4 D277 stood at Benfield Road. At 11.55am the 'Flying Scotsman' passed south in the charge of D272.

Saturday 29 October 1960

'A3' 'Pacific' No 60063 *Isinglass* was seen in Heaton Junction. Also Type 4 diesel D251 was seen heading south at 11.58am with the 'Flying Scotsman'.

'A3' No 60063 *Isinglass*. R. F. Orpwood, the Gresley Society

Saturday 12 November 1960

'A4' 'Pacific' No 60004 *William Whitelaw* was seen at around half past ten am heading north with a brake van. Another 'A4' No 60011 *Empire of India* stood in the Quarter-Mile for about three hours. I watched it all the time I had available. It looked in good condition. It stood quietly for about three hours, then the chime whistle was sounded and it moved away north with a goods train. As it did so, an 'A3' 'Pacific' No 60083 *Sir Hugo* passed light in the other direction. 'A1' 'Pacific' No 60151 *Midlothian* also passed south light. 'V2s' Nos 60842 and 60865 were sighted, both heading north. Type 4 diesels seen were Nos D243, D237 and D282, which was seen at night at Chillingham Road bridge heading a southbound train. [At Chillingham Road bridge there was a very tall NER signal box, Heaton South.]

Saturday 24 December 1960 Christmas Eve

'V2' No 60944 was seen coming into Heaton carriage sidings with a train of empty coaches. Type 4 D272 headed the down 'North Briton' to Glasgow at 11.45am. 'A3' 'Pacific' No 60100 *Spearmint* was seen heading for Newcastle on a passenger service. It was also seen later in the day heading north again. 'A4' No 60023 *Golden Eagle* was seen on the down Edinburgh 'Flying Scotsman'. 'V2' No 60801 headed north immediately afterwards on a train of tank wagons.

Thursday 29 December 1960

'A3' 'Pacific' No 60099 *Call Boy* was seen heading an Edinburgh-bound passenger north at approx 11.30am. As the air was clear and frosty it made a tremendous noise. The Glasgow-bound 'North Briton', headed by Type 4 diesel-electric D257, was seen at 11.40am. At 1.30pm 'A1' 'Pacific' No 60161 *North British* was headed north on a parcels

Opposite: 'V2' No 60916 heads a train of wagons north through Heaton Junction on 12 May 1962. The tall North Eastern Railway Heaton South signal box stands in the background by the Chillingham Road bridge. *R. F. Orpwood, the Gresley Society*

train. Later in the afternoon 'B1' Class No 61176 was seen on a short train of vans. Heading south light was 'Austerity' 'WD' 2-8-0 No 90016. Class 'A1' 'Pacific' No 60116 *Hal o'the Wynd* was seen heading south through Heaton with a long freight train.

Friday 30 December 1960

'A3' 'Pacific' No 60035 *Windsor Lad* was seen heading a Pullman train south into Newcastle at approx 2.30pm. It looked in splendid condition.

The 'Flying Scotsman' headed by Type 4 diesel D262 travelled north. Almost immediately afterwards 'V2' No 60964 *The Durham Light Infantry* started north with a train of tank wagons. Standing alone in Heaton yards was Type 4 diesel D241.

Above: 'A3' No 60035 *Windsor Lad*. *R. F. Orpwood, the Gresley Society*

Opposite: 'A4' No 60023 *Golden Eagle* at Gateshead MPD on 18 September 1963. *R. F. Orpwood, the Gresley Society*

Saturday 31 December 1960

2-8-0 No 90430 was seen in Heaton Junction on a freight train. A passenger headed north pulled by Type 4 diesel D256. Other diesel locomotives seen were Sulzer type locomotives D5105 and D5106, which were working south coupled together on a passenger train. Type 4 D274 headed south light. A Newcastle-bound freight headed by D266 passed me at Benton Bank. At Heaton Junction D278 was working a freight train into Newcastle. A passenger train headed to Newcastle pulled by D247. At Benton Bank a train of tank wagons headed north hauled by 'V2' No 60865. Other 'V2s' seen were Nos 60894, 60827, 60976. The northbound 'Flying Scotsman' was headed by 'A1' No 60154 *Bon Accord*, which was seen at Benton Bank. A passenger train was seen in the morning travelling north headed by 'A1' No 60137 *Redgauntlet*. A Newcastle-bound passenger from Edinburgh passed through headed by 'A4' No 60012 *Commonwealth of Australia*. 'B1' No 61351 was seen, as also were 'K3s' Nos 61917, 61930, 61906.

Thursday 5 January 1961
Central station, Newcastle-upon-Tyne

Seen at Newcastle Central today were the following locomotives. A Type 4 diesel-electric D265, which pulled in, headed south, on Platform 9. It soon uncoupled and an 'A3' 'Pacific' No 60051 *Blink Bonny* took over. This engine deafeningly blew off steam without ceasing. Then with a tremendous effort it heaved its eleven coaches out. Gresley 'V2' No 60895 was seen, as also was 'V2' No 60810. The green tank engine No 68723 also busied itself in the south end of the station [another sighting of one of the 'J72' NER station pilots]. Class 'K1' No 62050 was seen on a northbound freight. Class 'WD' No 90430 headed through the station towards Gateshead, light. Class 'B1' No 61338 was also seen on a freight train. A southbound passenger pulled into Platform 10 headed by Type 4 diesel D273. A north passenger also came in headed by diesel-electric D240.

January 5th 1961. Central Station. Newcastle

Seen at Newcastle Central today were the following locomotives. A Type 4 diesel electric no. D265 which pulled in, headed south, on platform 9. It soon uncoupled and an A3 pacific no. 60051 'Blink Bonny' took over. This engine flew off without ceasing. Then, with a tremendous effort it heaved its eleven coaches out. Gresley V2 no. 60845 was seen, as also was V2 no. 60810. V3 no. 67651 was in the station all afternoon as was no. 68680. The green tank engine no. 68723 also busied itself in the south end of the station. Class A1 no. 60020 was seen on a north freight. Class V2 no. 60420 headed through the station towards Gateshead, light. Class A1 no. 60138 was also seen on a freight train. A Southbound passenger pu-

-lled into platform 10, headed by Type 4 diesel no. D273. A North passenger also came in headed by diesel electric no. D260. This train was the train for the Tyne Commission quay. Meanwhile on platform 9 the southbound 'Queen of Scots' pullman, headed by A1 no. 60152 'Holyrood' pulled. This was relieved by A3 pacific no. 60036 'Colombo'. Amidst a turmoil of slipping, it drew slowly out. B1 no. 61387 was seen on a goods train. On a passenger train on the electrified lines was Type 4 diesel no. D306. The first Type 4 I have seen in the 300 number series. The North-bound 'Flying Scotsman' pulled into platform 9. It was headed by A4 pacific no. 60010 'Dominion of Canada'. From its cab belched clouds of grey

This train was the boat train for the Tyne Commission Quay. Meanwhile, on Platform 9 the southbound 'Queen of Scots' Pullman headed by 'A1' No 60152 *Holyrood* pulled in. This was relieved by 'A3' 'Pacific' No 60036 *Colombo*. Amidst a turmoil of slipping it drew slowly out. 'B1' No 61387 was seen on a goods train. On a passenger train on the electrified line was Type 4 diesel D306, the first Type 4 diesel I have seen in the 300 number series. [The 'electrified line' refers to the lines for the North Tyneside electric trains to the coast.]

The northbound 'Flying Scotsman' pulled into Platform 9. It was headed by 'A4' 'Pacific' No 60010 *Dominion of Canada*. From its cab belched clouds of grey smoke. The driver and fireman were compelled to hang out of the cab windows for air. It drew to a stop. The smoke continued to pour out of the cab. Steam sizzled from the safety valves, whistle and cylinders and it made a loud roar. The 'A4' hitched forward a little then went off to Gateshead sheds. It was relieved by Type 4 diesel D263, which moved away

A North Tyneside electric train for the coast stands at Newcastle Central on 3 September 1962. *R. F. Orpwood, the Gresley Society*

to Edinburgh. Then was seen a 9F 2-10-0 No 92199, which took the southbound lines on a freight train around the outside of the station. On Platform 8 a parcels train from the south came in headed by 'A1' No 60142 *Edward Fletcher*. At the same time a Birmingham train headed south drew to a halt in Platform 10. It was headed by 'A1' No 60116 *Hal o'the Wynd*.

[Diary entry: 'In the afternoon I went to the Central station. Saw piles of engines, including 'A4' No 60010 *Dominion of Canada*. That leaves only 5 more for me to get.' My final five at this stage, I remember, were *Andrew K. McCosh*, *Quicksilver*, *Mallard*, *Miles Beevor* and *Golden Fleece* – all London engines.]

Tuesday 10 January 1961
Carlisle Citadel Station

Seen at Carlisle station was 'A3' 'Pacific' No 60077 *The White Knight* in charge of the northbound 'Thames-Clyde Express'. Afterwards a 'Britannia' 'Pacific' came into Platform 3 heading a Liverpool-Glasgow train. It was No 70045 *Lord Rowallan*. It spurted steam from every available place. It took water and moved away amidst ear-splitting blasts of steam from the front, which I was compelled to stand away from. Then No 72007 *Clan Mackintosh* stood for a while by itself. Then a southbound train came in headed by a 'Coronation' 4-6-2, No 46241 *City of Edinburgh*. This uncoupled and was relieved by No 72007.

A Type 2 Sulzer Bo-Bo diesel D5079 pulled a passenger train into the station. Also, on freight duties, was 'A3' No 60089 *Felstead*. The southbound 'Royal Scot' came in headed by 'Coronation' No 46248 *City of Leeds*. This engine was in maroon livery. From the engine's front footsteps a wheel tapper picked up a dead pheasant that must have flown into the loco's path. He handed it to the fireman who threw it onto the tender. The southbound 'Mid-Day Scot' was headed by No 46227 *Duchess of Devonshire*. The same

'A3' No 60077 *The White Knight* at Gateshead MPD on 29 May 1964. *R. F. Orpwood, the Gresley Society*

train to the north was headed by No 46245 *City of London*, which stopped for only 2 mins to take water. This loco was in maroon livery, as far as I could see that is amidst bursts of steam and violent roars of smoke as the engine moved out. This was followed by No 72006 *Clan Mackenzie* in charge of a passenger. A southbound passenger pulled in in the charge of No 46229 *Duchess of Hamilton*, which was relieved by 'Jubilee' No 45716 *Swiftsure*. No 45729 *Furious* was seen in the station, light. Also seen was 'Royal Scot' Class No 46130 *The West Yorkshire Regiment* and also No 46145 *The Duke of Wellington's Regt (West Riding)*, which was travelling south.

Others seen: D297, D2, D2164, 63385, 61216, 65663, 61241 *Viscount Ridley*, 42833, 47492, 69155, 45479, 65480, 44900, 44324, 45716, 45326, 47288.

Also seen was a large steam breakdown crane coloured red, and made by Cowans and Sheldon Ltd of Carlisle. [Diary entry: 'Been to Carlisle. Stayed in station all the time. Saw *City of London*. Piles of Cities, Duchesses, Clans'. *City of London* is singled out for mention because at the time it was Hornby's new model version of the Stanier 'Pacific', which boys of my age coveted.]

The Ian Allan 'Combined Volume' for 1961, the last great year of steam, portraying steam's replacements on the cover.

Description of rail journey
Newcastle-Carlisle 10 January 1961

[My ventures to Carlisle and York, as recorded in this diary, were made in the company of an aunt who was North of England manager for Empire Stores' station kiosks (long gone), which sold fruit and confectionery. On some of her regular travels I would accompany her and be left trainspotting all day while she attended to business.]

The journey was made in a six-car diesel train on 10 January. The train left Newcastle Central at exactly 10.30am. We quickly accelerated through Elswick yards giving a short blast on the horn. Scotswood was passed at 47mph. The train moved quickly by the works of Vickers-Armstrong and into sight of the river. Then the brakes were applied and we came to a stop. After about 6 mins we started off again, passed Deleval Box and entered a short tunnel. Stella North Power Station and Walbottle were passed at 30mph. Speed increased to 50mph near Ryton, but dropped to 30 as we ran parallel with the Tyne. North Wylam was quickly passed, and the Tyne was crossed by way of a high metal bridge. Then we came into sight of Prudhoe where long lines of hopper and mineral wagons stood in sidings. A steady 48mph was kept up, and increased to 51 as we sped through Riding Mill. The brakes were then applied and the horn sounded. Corbridge was passed at 35mph and we came to a halt at Hexham at 11.05am, 35 mins after we had left Newcastle.

After a stop of 4 minutes we left Hexham and approached Fourstones. This was passed at 53mph. Here the River Tyne runs parallel with the railway on the left. The brakes were again applied and a short stop was made at Haydon Bridge at 11.20am. After Haydon Bridge the Tyne swerves away to the right and then to the left again. It is crossed by numerous small bridges. Along this stretch the train's speed was reduced to 25mph and Haltwhistle was reached. Starting off again we passed a large black van with a snowplough on the front.

It had a code name 'Shark'. The speed quickly increased and Gilsland was passed at 60mph. There followed a long fast stretch where the line winds into open country. Speed moved from 65.5 to 70, then to 71mph. Then the diesel braked to 50mph and we passed Brampton Junction. We sped through Heads Nook at 60 and Wetheral at 30. Carlisle came into sight. We passed through Carlisle goods yards at 40mph and came to a halt at Carlisle station at 12.01pm.

[Here follows in the diary a brief attempt at scene setting. There are inaccuracies, but the account is basically correct.]

The Central Station, Newcastle-on-Tyne, is situated on the main London to Edinburgh line. It provides a stop for all the crack East Coast expresses, except for the well-known non-stop 'Elizabethan' service. The main line to the north is on Platform 8, and to the south on Platforms 9 and 10, while the electric services to Tynemouth and Whitley Bay are on Platforms 5 and 6. A train leaving Newcastle for the north first wends its way slowly through the complicated trackwork to Manors station. Here the electrified lines for Gosforth and Jesmond take a sharp curve to the left. Once Manors station is passed, the train passes under Newbridge Street and picks its way through Byker and thence to Heaton. A long stretch of track is ahead, and up to Heaton Station a gradient of about 1 in 200 is encountered. Once past Heaton sheds a gentle curve takes the train towards the north, while the Whitley Bay and Tynemouth electric services swerve to the right. An engine's whistle is always sounded here and the speed increased.

The track begins to straighten out and the Scottish goods sidings are passed. Once through here a train comes to Benton Box and climbs a slight incline. Once over the bridge at Benfield Road, about half a mile from Heaton sheds, the train is out of Newcastle and speed increases. All the famous East Coast trains pass along this stretch, including the 'Flying Scotsman', 'Elizabethan', 'Talisman', 'Heart of Midlothian'

Heaton Station, now demolished, in July 1970.

An NER notice at Gateshead, photographed on 2 May 1964. *R. F. Orpwood, the Gresley Society*

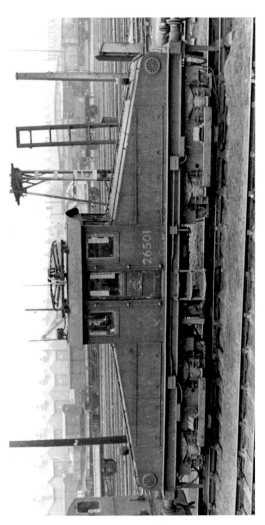

Class ES1 Bo-Bo electric locomotive No 26501 at Heaton MPD on 14 May 1961. Together with its twin No 26500, it worked, both by overhead and third rail, on trains from the Newcastle Quayside branch. *R. F. Orpwood, the Gresley Society*

61

and 'Queen of Scots' Pullman. The locomotives are mostly 'A3s' and 'A4s', 'V2s', 'A1s' and 'A2s'. The streamlined 'A4s' are usually from Gateshead (52A) and Edinburgh (64B). King's Cross (34A) 'A4s' hardly ever venture north of Newcastle, except on the non-stop 'Elizabethan' service in July, August and September. They usually stay overnight at Haymarket shed, Edinburgh, and return to London the following day.

Saturday 4 February 1961

[Diary entry: 'Been into town for *Trains Illustrated*. Watched Benny Hill in his new series. Fabulous.' Here my diary for 1961 ceases. Interesting early use of 'Fabulous', a word more associated with a slightly later period perhaps, for example 'The Fab Four'.]

Snow has been falling and is making the tracks slippery. Seen on a down passenger was 'A1' No 60137 *Redgauntlet*. Also in Heaton Junction was 'B1' Class No 61099. 'A3' No 60091 *Captain Cuttle* was seen on a down freight. Bad rail conditions caused it to slip a lot before it began to accelerate. Booked on the down 'Flying Scotsman' was 'A4' No 60019 *Bittern*. Also on a down freight was 'A2' No 60530 *Sayajirao*.

Opposite: An NER slotted-post signal at Heaton MPD, 29 May 1964. R. F. Orpwood, the Gresley Society

Above: Ian Allan's *Locoshed Book*, listing the shed allocations of all BR locomotives.

'A3' No 60091 *Captain Cuttle* at Gateshead MPD.

Another portrait of *Captain Cuttle* at Heaton MPD on 29 May 1964. *R. F. Orpwood, the Gresley Society*

Bittern, the 'A4', was picking up speed quickly at Benton Bank. It could have been cleaner. However, No 60530 was in splendid condition. Perhaps it had just been cleaned. It slowly picked its way forward. Then the driver slowly opened the regulator. A fearful fit of slipping followed due to the greasy condition of the track. The wheels began to grip again and the engine soon began to accelerate.

Benfield Road bridge has now been completely renovated. It has been given new girders and the embankment has been reinforced with high walls. It was learned yesterday that the 'Deltic' diesel locomotives for the East Coast route will be in service soon, and they are to be named. The LNER is going to continue its classic racehorse names (which won't be so bad seeing that we may lose the 'A3s'). The NER has selected regimental names (very disappointing from my point of view), and the Scottish Region has chosen birds.

It has come to my notice that the 'J72' No 68682 was withdrawn in March last year. The reason for my mention of this is that it happened to be the first locomotive I 'spotted'. It used to be allocated to Heaton sheds, and then was transferred to Tweedmouth. I know this as I saw it at Berwick whilst returning from Edinburgh by rail. Locos 'A3' No 60104 *Solario* and 'A2' No 60509 *Waverley* have been withdrawn. Another class that has disappeared is the 'D30', and also one class is rapidly disappearing, the 'D49s'.

[No 68682 was an engine notorious for obscuring the view from the Marleen Avenue vantage point. Almost invariably it would start to shunt a long train of vans and wagons just as a speeding express came by in the background. It may even have been this locomotive or one of its class, as I seem to recall, that provides my earliest railway recollection of all. As a very small boy, in the company of an aunt, I remember gazing up at a tank locomotive on the 'Quarter-Mile' sidings and its driver calling down from the embankment and offering to give me a ride in its cab.

'J72' No 68680 at Newcastle Central on 11 March 1960. *R. F. Orpwood, the Gresley Society*

In *Kiddar's Luck*, Jack Common gives an account of just such an episode in Heaton Junction, describing it as 'one of the utterly-unexpected tremendous gestures my father used to make just once in a way'.

I would like to think that maybe the following story he tells involved No 68682, a long-time Heaton resident. My own experience seems to be in direct line of descent from Jack Common's when he describes how he was invited to ride with his engine-driver father at Heaton Junction earlier in the century:

He was running a shunting engine at this time, and often coming from school, I would hang around the big gate of the yard with some of my pals proudly pointing out his operations to them. He must have seen me, but instead of putting an instant embargo on the practice, which must have been his first idea, I bet, one evening he stepped down from the engine-cab and strolled towards me, calling me to come to him. I hung back, naturally; my pals got ready to run. Several times he called. I answered only with an uneasy 'What?' At last I thought it safest to take a few steps towards him. He reached forward, picked me up, and said easily, 'Come on, I'll give you a ride.'

I hardly dared believe that he could actually mean I was to ride on an authentic locomotive, but a glance back at my two little pals standing so quiet and awed, forlorn at being left out of such a miraculous treat, certainly indicated that it really was going to happen. It did, too. Almost stupefied with the wondrous rarity of the event, I found myself climbing up steep, metal steps, hauled in by my father's mate, and here I was close to the great steam pulse, passing by the fire-box and hoisted on to the driver's seat with the caution to keep my head in whenever an inspector came by. You see, the whole thing was illegal: that was another knock-out. You couldn't imagine such a one as my father breaking railway rules. Not that I feared for him, mind you (I took the inspector story as largely kid-ball) but it was so unlikely that he'd make this vast enlargement of the very fabric of life merely for the sake of amusing me.

Well, it was a terrific evening. All were agreed, whether it was the driver, the fireman or one of the shunters hopping on to the engine step, that now I was on the railway I must earn my keep. The fireman, pretending to be tired, handed me his shovel – I struggled to get a lump or two clear of the fire-box door into the fanning heat of caked flame behind; the driver instructed me how to pull the whistle chain when he gave the word – I got some strangulated blasts out of it which I could only hope the signalmen and shunters knew how to interpret; and all our visitors were insistent that I should keep my eye continually on the gauges, that was most important – I watched the water-level fluctuating in the glass-tube and duly reported any major change. While I was so busy, the little side-tanker was usually trundling along, banging into a row of trucks, or reversing and trailing one of them with a great rattle over a series of points, for the complicated operations of shunting were in full progress. My head was often bumped against the side of the cab, but I was so occupied in trying to follow all the moves made and the many instructions I was given to watch this and look out for that, I noticed no minor discomforts. Not even the flight of time. Presently, we ran out on a far line near the big gate and stopped. The engine settled down to a regular sighing; the fireman got out a clean bucket and started washing his hands. Looking out, at a quite unfamiliar view of the houses on Chillingham Road, it surprised me to see they were in such a sudden darkness and that a young moon, bright as a razor, was ready to drop among their chimney-pots.]

Monday 13 February 1961

Seen today light at Benfield Road was 'V2' No 60835 *The Green Howard, Alexandra Princess of Wales's Own Yorkshire Regiment*. On the up 2.15pm Pullman was 'A4' No 60011 *Empire of India*. As it passed it gave a loud blast on its chime whistle. It was seen again later in the day at Heaton Carriage Sidings, probably before travelling back to Edinburgh on a freight train. A 'V2' No 60951 was seen heading a train of three cattle wagons northwards. Type 4 diesel-electric D270 headed the up 'Heart of Midlothian' into Newcastle at approx 4.00pm.

Wednesday 15 February 1961

At Benfield Road the bridge has been repaired. New girders have been put in. Today a girder was being loaded onto Bogie Bolster and Double Bolster wagons coupled up. A diesel 0-6-0 shunting engine was in charge, No 13317. When operations were over, a number of locomotives followed each other, light, in a line onto the bridge to test it for load bearing. They were 'V2' No 60978, 'B1' No 61246 *Lord Balfour of Burleigh*, Type 4 1-Co-Co-1 diesel D247, and on another track came 'A1' No 60132 *Marmion*.

Later a Gresley 'A3' No 60083 *Sir Hugo* came south towards Newcastle light engine. The 2.25pm Pullman was headed by 'A3' No 60043 *Brown Jack*.

Another passenger was headed into Newcastle by 'A3' No 60101 *Cicero*. The 'Heart of Midlothian' was headed by Type 4 D257, and the northbound 'North Briton' was headed by D250.

Opposite: 'A1' No 60132 *Marmion* at Heaton MPD on 29 May 1962.
R. F. Orpwood, the Gresley Society

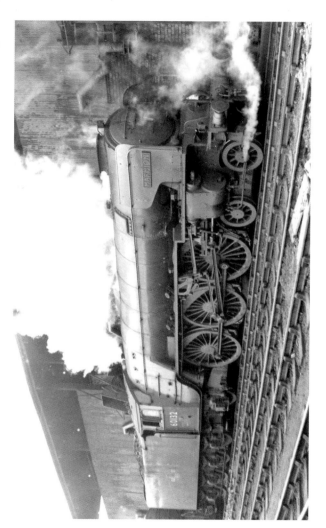

71

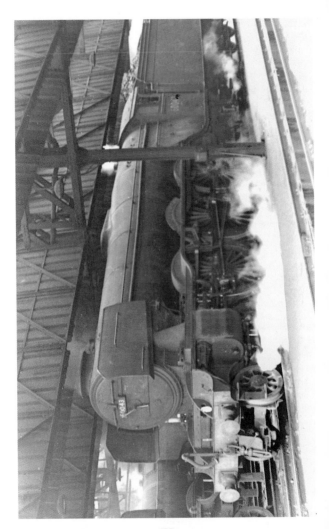

72

Saturday 18 February 1961

'V2' No 60860 *Durham School* was seen on a down freight starting from the Quarter-Mile. Another interesting working was a work train in Heaton Junction. Engine No 64865 headed a 'Newcastle Civil Engineers' steam crane, plus a blue workmen's van, plus a goods brake van, into a siding at Heaton Junction. Type 4 D251 headed a freight train into Newcastle. Then Type 4 D257 headed the down 'North Briton'.

The next locomotive seen was Type 4 D264 on a northbound parcels train. An unusual working was an Ivatt taper boiler locomotive introduced in 1946, No 46479, coupled to 'J27' 65799, both moving south. At around 1.00pm a Type 4 headed a 'Condor' cross Benfield Road at a good speed. A 'V2' 60865 headed a five-coach passenger train through Heaton Junction. It was picking up speed quickly and was rocking violently, as also was its tender. This is a very powerful type of engine for such a light train. My guess is that it was returning home to Scotland and it was given this train instead of returning home light (a waste of power).

'A4' No 60011 *Empire of India* headed a northbound passenger train in the afternoon. This particular locomotive has been doing quite a lot of working around this district. Another northbound freight train started from a standstill in the Quarter-Mile. It was headed by 'A3' No 60058 *Blair Athol*. Finally 'A3' No 60073 *St Gatien* was seen at Benfield Road.

Opposite: 'A3' No 60043 *Brown Jack* at Heaton MPD on 5 June 1963. R. F. Orpwood, the Gresley Society

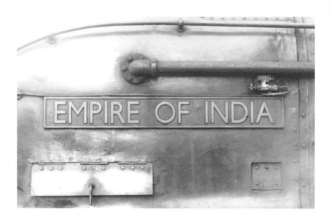

'A4' No 60011 *Empire of India. R. F. Orpwood, the Gresley Society*

The crest carried by No 60011:'Heaven's Light Our Guide'. *R. F. Orpwood, the Gresley Society*

Friday 17 March 1961
Central station, Newcastle-upon-Tyne

Seen on a southbound train was 'A3' No 60058 *Blair Athol*. A freight train was pulled in from the south by 'A1' No 60147 *North Eastern*. A southbound freight was seen with a Bo-Bo diesel-electric No D5149 on front. The afternoon Pullman to the south was brought in by 'A3' No 60097 *Humorist* (fitted with smoke deflectors). This was taken over by 'A3' No 60074 *Harvester*.

The northbound 'Flying Scotsman' was brought into Newcastle by Type 4 diesel D208. This was taken over by D261. 'V2s' seen were Nos 60835 and 60829. No 92182 pulled a southbound freight. A similar train was headed to the south by 'A1' No 60132 *Marmion*.

Wednesday 22 March 1961

'A4' No 60011 *Empire of India* on a northbound passenger train late afternoon.

Friday 7 April 1961

Seen in Heaton Junction: a 'Matisa' ballast tamping machine. There hasn't been one in the small siding since last summer (colour: yellow). It had a notice on it: 'Do not watch this machine. Watch your own safety.' [I love the literacy of such notices, which are peculiarly English, as for example once at Victoria Station: 'You are requested not to feed the pigeons; they have been causing a nuisance at this station, as many passengers will know to their discomfort'. Near my home in Cambridge, as I write, there is a notice by the River Cam: 'You are requested not to feed bread to the wildfowl. It is not healthy for them, and may do them more harm than good'.]

Type 4 diesel D273 was speeding south light. Also seen 'V2' No 60976.

Signals were up both ways. The northbound 'Queen of Scots' Pullman headed by 'A4' No 60031 *Golden Plover* was passed by a southbound passenger in the charge of 'A4' No 60004 *William Whitelaw*.

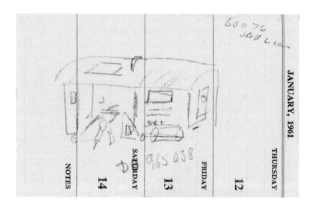

My little sketch, done in situ, of ballast tamper DB965038.

Monday 10 April 1961
Central station, Newcastle-upon-Tyne

A Birmingham-Newcastle train was pulled in by 'A2/3' 'Pacific' No 60516 *Hycilla* (50A). On the opposite platform a Type 4 diesel D235 (8A) pulled a passenger train in. A Bo-Bo diesel D5109 was employed on light freight duties in the station. The 1.25pm Edinburgh-King's Cross train was in the charge of 'A4' streamlined 'Pacific' No 60011 *Empire of India*. This was relieved by 'A1' 'Pacific' No 60159 *Bonnie Dundee*, which pulled the train out in the opposite direction over the High Level Bridge and not by the more usual King Edward Bridge. Another Bo-Bo diesel-electric was D5707, which passed south, light, on the outside of the station. A freight to the north was seen in the charge of No 61176 (51A).

During the last week the 'Queen of Scots' Pullman has been hauled by 'A4' 'Pacific' No 60031 *Golden Plover*. It pulls the train from Edinburgh to Newcastle and then takes it back later in the afternoon. Today was no exception. *Golden Plover* came in looking in splendid condition.

A man was at the platform with a miniature tape recorder recording operations. The 'A4' uncoupled and was relieved by 'A3' No 60036 *Colombo*. The train pulled out and I noticed that it was partly composed of the new steel Pullman cars, 'Pearl', 'Snipe', 'Stork', etc.

The down 'Flying Scotsman' was brought in by 'A4' 'Pacific' No 60006 *Sir Ralph Wedgwood*. It was relieved by D262. The 'Heart of Midlothian' was brought in by diesel D237 and relieved by D274. This was followed by a southbound freight in the charge of 'A2/3' No 60512 *Steady Aim*. Also seen was D273.

Later, 'A4' No 60031 *Golden Plover* was again seen returning to Edinburgh on the 'Queen of Scots'. It was passed by the up 'Talisman' in the charge of 'A4' No 60004 *William Whitelaw*.

'A4' No 60031 *Golden Plover*. R. F. Orpwood, the Gresley Society

Wednesday 12 April 1961

'A3' No 60052 *Prince Palatine* headed north on a passenger train in the evening.

Friday 14 April 1961

A number of interesting workings were seen. The 'Queen of Scots', instead of being in the charge of 'A4' No 60031 *Golden Plover*, was in the charge of 'A4' No 60011 *Empire of India*, another commonly seen 'A4'. *Golden Plover* had worked a passenger train north a couple of hours beforehand. 'A4' No 60004 *William Whitelaw* had charge of the southbound 'Talisman'.

A 'Matisa' ballast tamping machine was seen working at Heaton sheds and was later driven to its usual siding. Also seen was 'A1' No 60132 *Marmion* on a north freight. The northbound 'North Briton' was headed by Type 4 diesel D266. 'V2' No 60971 headed a train composed entirely of 'Conflat' wagons. Another 'V2' seen was No 60913.

Saturday 15 April 1961

Observed was No 90417. Also a long freight headed north by 'A2' 'Pacific' No 60521 *Watling Street*. A southbound freight was seen in the charge of 'V2' No 60922. 'A3' 'Pacific' No 60100 *Spearmint* was light engine in the Quarter-Mile sidings.

[No 60100 *Spearmint* was made famous on the East Coast Main Line by the celebrated Scottish top-link engine driver Norman McKillop, who wrote eloquently about his experiences with it as his regular locomotive in *Enginemen Elite* (1958).]

Diesel D241 headed the northbound 'North Briton'. 'V2' No 60860 *Durham School* had charge of a short passenger train to the north. An 'A3' was heading the 'Queen of Scots' Pullman instead of the usual 'A4'. It was No 60043 *Brown Jack*. Other locos seen: 'V2s' 60977, 60802, 60910, 60891.

'A3' No 60100 *Spearmint. R. F. Orpwood, the Gresley Society*

Finally, 'A3' No 60052 *Prince Palatine* was seen in the Quarter-Mile' sidings.

Three more 'A2' 'Pacifics' have been withdrawn: Nos 60504 *Mons Meg*, 60507 *Highland Chieftain*, 60510 *Robert the Bruce*.

Age 15
1961-62

Saturday 17 June 1961
[Includes my first ever sighting of a 'Deltic' (interestingly without comment) – the locomotives that were very soon to put an end forever to the glory of the steam era on the East Coast Main Line.]

The 'Elizabethan' trains were headed by 'A4' No 60031 *Golden Plover* and by King's Cross 'A4' No 60014 *Silver Link*.

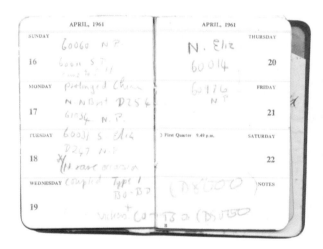

'A4' No 60031 *Golden Plover* on the 'S. Eliz' and 'A4' No 60014 *Silver Link* on the 'N. Eliz' are clearly marked in a diary for 1961 being used as my spotter's notebook. 'A4' No 60011 *Empire of India* is recorded as giving a 'prolonged chime' whistle as it passed through Heaton.

Also seen on a southbound passenger train, and then later in the day on a northbound train, was 'A3' No 60096 *Papyrus*.

Production series 'Deltic' D9004 had the southbound 'Flying Scotsman'. 'A3' No 60095 *Flamingo* is withdrawn. [Two ominous sentences.]

Also seen on a northbound passenger 'A4' No 60002 *Sir Murrough Wilson*. Six 'Deltics' are destined for Gateshead.

The nameplate of 'A3' No 60095 *Flamingo*, the second of its class to be scrapped. *R. F. Orpwood, the Gresley Society*

Saturday 1 July 1961

'A4' No 60004 *William Whitelaw* worked a special train north ahead of the 'Elizabethan', which had 'A4' No 60031 *Golden Plover*. 'A3' No 60070 *Gladiateur* was observed heading north. The northbound 'Flying Scotsman' had 'A2' No 60534 *Irish Elegance*. 'A1' No 60151 *Midlothian* and 'V2' No 60805 were on passenger duties. D347 had the northbound 'Queen of Scots' Pullman.

82

Saturday 22 July 1961

'A3' 'Pacific' No 60060 *The Tetrarch* was seen headed north on a passenger train. 'A4' No 60011 *Empire of India* cruised a passenger train southbound through the junction and, after a long sound on its chime whistle, was brought to a halt at Heaton sheds by signals. Type 4 diesel D254 had the northbound 'North Briton'. This was followed by a short passenger train in the charge of 'B1' No 61034 *Chiru*. The southbound 11.50am 'Elizabethan' was in the charge of Haymarket 'A4' No 60031 *Golden Plover*, which seems to be the regular engine. However, King's Cross has provided two 'A4s' to share the working, Nos 60014 and 60028. Today the northbound 'Elizabethan' had 'A4' No 60014 *Silver Link*. Two northbound passengers were headed by Type 4 D247 and 'V2' No 60976 respectively. A very unusual sight took place. Coupled together and travelling north were a Vickers Type D5000 series Bo-Bo diesel and a Type 1 D8000 series Bo-Bo diesel.

Observations made during my summer holidays in Malborough, Devon 1961

[For me, journeying in those days from Newcastle to Devon was almost like going abroad. And the prospect of travelling by direct train, and of seeing classes of locomotive I had only ever seen pictures of, or read about, was much more exciting than the holiday itself. The journey I recall took almost 12 hours.]

Up journey

Our train on the Newcastle-Newton Abbot run was headed as follows:

Newcastle-Sheffield: a 'V2'.
Sheffield-Cheltenham: a 'Jubilee' 45000 series.
Cheltenham-Gloucester-Bristol: Sulzer 1-Co-Co-1 diesel D79.
Bristol-Newton Abbot: 'Warship' diesel-hydraulic.

Opposite: 'A3' No 60060 *The Tetrarch* at Heaton MPD on 5 June 1963. 'A3' No 60088 *Book Law* is to the right. *R. F. Orpwood, the Gresley Society*

Down journey

Kingsbridge-Brent: diesel railcar W55019.

Brent-Newton Abbot: 'Warship' diesel-hydraulic D839 *Relentless* and 'Hall' Class steam locomotive No 6914 *Langton Hall* working together.

Newton Abbot-Bristol: No 5020 *Trematon Castle*. [I can still vividly remember what a thrill it was to be travelling for the first time behind a 'Castle'.]

Bristol-Sheffield: 'Jubilee' No 45690 *Leander*.

Sheffield-York: 'Jubilee' No 45664 *Nelson*.

York-Newcastle: two Sulzer diesels working together.

Locomotives observed: up journey

At Gateshead sheds: two Type 5 'Deltics' [it's interesting that I don't bother to record their numbers], 'A3' No 60041 *Salmon Trout*, 'A3' No 60091 *Captain Cuttle*, 'A2' No

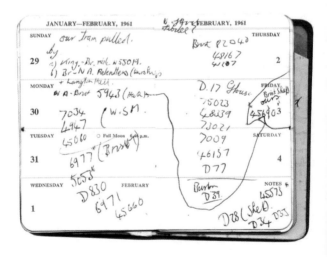

My notebook for loco numbers recorded during the summer holiday in Devon in 1961.

60529 *Pearl Diver*, 'A4' Nos 60011 *Empire of India*, 60018 *Sparrow Hawk*, 60023 *Golden Eagle*, 'Britannia' Class No 70038 *Robin Hood*.

At Darlington: Type 1 Bo-Bo D8077, 'V2' No 60809 *The Snapper, The East Yorkshire Regiment, The Duke of York's Own*.

At York: 'V2' Nos 60930, 60960, 60943, 'A4' No 60030 *Golden Fleece*, 'A2' No 60515 *Sun Stream*, Type 4s D349, D284, D102.

At Moorthorpe: Type 1 diesels D8002, D8069, D8064, D8057, D8063.

At Sheffield: 'Jubilee' Class No 45594 *Bhopal*, 8F 2-8-0s 48033, 48261.

At Derby: Type 2 4-6-0 No 46440, Type 5 4-6-0 No 73074, 8F 2-8-0 Nos 48124, 48640, 48351, also 3F 0-6-T No 47643 and 'Royal Scot' No 46148 *The Manchester Regiment*.

At Birmingham: 8F 2-8-0 Nos 48128, 48350, Type 1 'North British' Class D8405, Type 4 D89.

At Bristol: 'Castle' Class 4-6-0 Nos 5036 *Lyonshall Castle*, 5026 *Criccieth Castle*, No 46106 *Gordon Highlander*, 'Warship' diesel-hydraulics D822 *Hercules*, D846 *Steadfast*, Type 1 D8472, No 46525, 'Hall' Class Nos 6958 *Oxburgh Hall*, 5950 *Wardley Hall*.

At Exeter: 'Warship' D868 *Zephyr*.

At Taunton: '4300' Class No 6372, No 4955 *Plaspower Hall*, 'Battle of Britain' 'Pacific' No 34068 *Kenley*, 'N' Class No 31842.

Locomotives observed: down journey

At Weston-super-Mare: No 7034 *Ince Castle*, No 4947 *Nanhoran Hall*, Class 5 4-6-0 No 45060.

At Totnes were seen two 'Warship' diesels coupled together: D828 *Magnificent* and D869 *Zest*. Also seen D852 *Tenacious*.

At Exeter: No 34079 *141 Squadron*.

At Taunton: No 4932 *Hatherton Hall*, No 7015 *Carn Brea Castle*.

At Bristol: No 6977 *Grundisburgh Hall*, No 5053 *Earl Cairns*, No 6971 *Athelhampton Hall*, 'Warship' D830 *Majestic*, No 45660 *Rooke*. Others seen here: Class 3 2-6-2T No 82040: 8F 2-8-0 No 48167, Class 2 2-6-2T No 41207.
At Gloucester: Type 4 D17, No 75023, 8F 2-8-0 No 48339, No 73021, No 7009 *Athelney Castle*, No 46137 *The Prince of Wales's Volunteers (South Lancashire)*, Type 4 D77.
At Burton-on-Trent: Type 4 D39.
At Sheffield: D28, D34, D33, No 45573 *Newfoundland*.
On the York-Newcastle run 'A2' No 60524 *Herringbone* passed in the opposite direction.

Saturday 12 August 1961

Two new 'A4' 'Pacifics' are on the 'Elizabethan': King's Cross 'Pacific' No 60030 *Golden Fleece* replaces No 60014 *Silver Link* and No 60028 *Walter K. Whigham*. And Haymarket 'A4' No 60024 *Kingfisher* replaces No 60031 *Golden Plover*. The trains today, north and southbound, were headed by Nos 60024 and 60030 respectively.

'V2' No 60929 headed a north passenger train, as also did D238, D239, 'V2' No 60900 and 'A3' No 60060 *The Tetrarch*. The southbound 'Queen of Scots' Pullman had Type 4 D242, while the 'Heart of Midlothian' southbound had Type 5 'Deltic' D9000.

Monday 14 August 1961

'A1' 'Pacific' No 60143 *Sir Walter Scott* was seen on a northbound passenger train. Type 4 diesel D282 had the 'North Briton'. The southbound 'Elizabethan' came through at approx 12.50pm in the charge of 'A4' No 60030 *Golden Fleece*.

'A4' No 60030 *Golden Fleece*. R. F. Orpwood, the Gresley Society

Tuesday 15 August 1961

Type 4 D246 headed a southbound passenger in advance of the northbound 'Elizabethan' in the charge of 'A4' No 60030 *Golden Fleece* at 2.05pm approx.

Type 4 D346 had the south 'Queen of Scots' Pullman. 'A1' 'Pacific' No 60124 *Kenilworth* was observed on a southbound freight, as also was Type 4 D261 on a train of container wagons. Type 5 'Deltic' D9006 had a north passenger, as also did No 61917, which was followed by No 61952 on a northbound freight.

Wednesday 16 August 1961

The 'North Briton' again had Type 4 D282, as also had the southbound 'Elizabethan' 'A4' No 60030 *Golden Fleece*. Others observed were 'A2' No 60538 *Velocity*, Type 4 D346 on the north 'Queen of Scots' and 'A3' No 60101 *Cicero* on a southbound fitted fish train. D5100 was observed in Heaton Junction.

Thursday 17 August 1961

'A4' No 60009 *Union of South Africa* had the up 'Elizabethan' instead of No 60024 *Kingfisher*. 'A4' No 60030 *Golden Fleece* had the down 'Elizabethan' at 2.10pm

'A4' No 60004 *William Whitelaw* stood in the Quarter-Mile for about three-quarters of an hour during which I was able to observe a great deal of it. It was on a northbound freight. Type 4 D238 had a southbound passenger train with two Royal Mail cars. 'A1' No 60143 *Sir Walter Scott* had the southbound 'Queen of Scots' Pullman.

'A4' No 60004 *William Whitelaw*. R. F. Orpwood, the Gresley Society

Friday 18 August 1961
Central station, Newcastle-upon-Tyne

'A1' No 60142 *Edward Fletcher* was observed on a southbound passenger. The ex- Edinburgh 'Talisman' was brought in by 'A3' No 60076 *Galopin* and relieved by 'A4' No 60020 *Guillemot* (52A).

Type 4 D349 had a northbound passenger. Type 4 D280 brought in the 'Anglo-Scottish Car-Carrier' and 'A1' No 60127 *Wilson Worsdell* relieved it (north).

A King's Cross-bound passenger came in headed by Type 4 D265. 'A4' 'Pacific' No 60026 *Miles Beevor* relieved it. 'V2' No 60975 was observed light. A southbound passenger train had 'A1' No 60154 *Bon Accord*. The northbound non-stop 'Elizabethan' in the charge of 'A4' No 60009 *Union of South Africa* made an unofficial stop of about 20 seconds at Platform 9 for some unknown reason. Type 4 D346 brought in and headed out the southbound 'Queen of Scots' Pullman. Likewise did D272 with the northbound 'Flying Scotsman'. 'A4' No 60029 *Woodcock* (34A) brought in a train from the south .

Opposite: 'A3' No 60076 *Galopin* at Gateshead MPD on 3 September 1962. R. F. Orpwood, the Gresley Society

Above: 'A4' No 60020 *Guillemot. R. F. Orpwood, the Gresley Society*

Above: 'A4' No 60029 *Woodcock. R. F. Orpwood, the Gresley Society*

The southbound 'Anglo-Scottish Car-Carrier' was headed by 'A3' No 60078 *Night Hawk* and was relieved by D280.

An Edinburgh-bound train had 'A1' No 60124 *Kenilworth* and was relieved by 'A3' No 60037 *Hyperion*. 'A2' No 60522 *Straight Deal* had a southbound passenger, as did Type 4 D252. D326 had a passenger train also.

A northbound passenger was seen in the charge of D241. The southbound 'Heart of Midlothian' was brought in by 'A3' No 60060 *The Tetrarch* and headed out by 'A3' No 60063 *Isinglass*, which was fitted with German-type smoke deflectors. An Edinburgh-bound train came into the station with 'A1' No 60138 *Boswell* on the front. This locomotive was relieved by 'A3' No 60051 *Blink Bonny*. Type 5 'Deltic' D9008 was headed light on its way to Gateshead sheds. A northbound passenger was observed in the charge of D242 and headed out by D265. D326 brought in a southbound passenger and gave way to 'A2' No 60512 *Steady Aim*. Finally, 'A1' No 60116 *Hal o'the Wynd* brought in a southbound passenger train.

Saturday 19 August 1961

Type 4 D238 was seen with a northbound passenger, as also was 'V2' No 60811. 'A4' 'Pacific' No 60009 *Union of South Africa* was on the southbound 'Elizabethan' at 11.55am. 'Deltic' D9010 was on a southbound passenger. 'A4' 'Pacific' No 60016 *Silver King* was observed at Heaton. It backed out of the sheds and made for the Central.

It was observed about 20 minutes later on a northbound passenger train. 'A2' No 60539 *Bronzino* had the southbound 'Talisman'. 'A1' No 60116 *Hal o'the Wynd* had the south 'Heart of Midlothian', and 'A1' No 60155 *Borderer* had a south passenger. 'V2' No 60937 passed south with a short train of cattle wagons, as also did 'V2' No 60910 light.

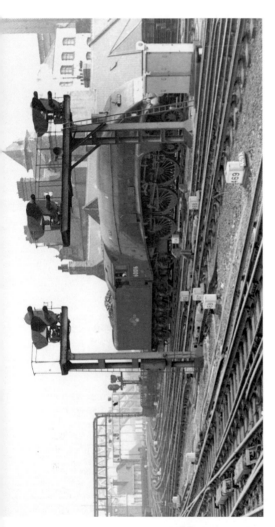

Above: 'A4' No 60016 *Silver King* approaches Newcastle Central from the direction of the High Level Bridge on 3 September 1962. *R. F. Orpwood, the Gresley Society*

Below: 'A1' No 60155 *Borderer* arrives at Newcastle Central at about 10.00pm with a train from Manchester on 29 May 1964. *R. F. Orpwood, the Gresley Society*

Friday 25 August 1961
Central station, Newcastle-upon-Tyne

First seen was 'A3' No 60076 *Galopin* on the northbound 'Talisman'. A north freight had 'V2' No 60891 immediately after this. Type 4 diesel D285 had a Birmingham train. Type 4 D290 brought in a passenger train and later went out on one. Type 4 D280 brought in the 'Anglo-Scottish Car-Carrier' (north) and was relieved by 'A4' No 60020 *Guillemot*. Type 5 'Deltic' D9006 brought in a southbound passenger and was relieved by 'A4' No 60002 *Sir Murrough Wilson*.

D9006 later relieved D272 with a King's Cross-Glasgow train. Type 4 D256 was on a south passenger and Type 4 D346 was in charge of the London-bound 'Queen of Scots' Pullman. 'A4' 'Pacific' No 60014 *Silver Link* (back on the 'Elizabethan') worked straight through to the north. This was followed by 'A4' No 60013 *Dominion of New Zealand*, which, instead of the usual chime whistle, gave a deep siren-type sound. The southbound 'Anglo-Scottish Car-Carrier' was headed in by 'A1' No 60147 *North Eastern* and relieved by D280. 'A2' No 60516 *Hycilla* had a Penzance

'A4' No 60002 *Sir Murrough Wilson*. R. F. Orpwood, the Gresley Society

train. 'A3' 'Pacific' No 60060 *The Tetrarch* was relieved of a northbound passenger by 'A1' No 60143 *Sir Walter Scott*.

Type 4 D290 had a Liverpool train, from which city came in D308. D351 was also noted on a southbound passenger. Finally, the southbound 'Heart of Midlothian', running 10 minutes late, was brought in by 'A3' No 60072 *Sunstar* and headed out by 'A2' No 60522 *Straight Deal*.

Tuesday 29 August 1961
York Central station

Our train from Newcastle was headed by Bo-Bo diesel-electric D5148, and from York back to Newcastle by D5149 of the same class.

At York sheds on the up journey were seen Type 4s D74, D355, D261, 'V2s' Nos 60800 *Green Arrow* and 60981, 61961, 62035, 62059, 62055, 43076.

'A4' No 60009 *Union of South Africa* is recorded on the 'S. Liz' (southbound 'Elizabethan') and 'A4' No 60030 *Golden Fleece* on the 'N. Liz' (northbound) during this visit to York station on 29 August 1961. The elaborate scribble probably reflects a 'fallow' period between trains.

In the station itself, the first locomotive seen was Type 5 'Deltic' D9002 on a Newcastle-King's Cross train. On a southbound stopping passenger was 'B1' No 61015 *Duiker*. 'A4' No 60020 *Guillemot* (52A) had a southbound passenger, as also 'A1' No 60116 *Hal o'the Wynd*.

The northbound 'North Briton' had Type 4 D284. Type 4 D258 had a Cardiff train. Other Type 4s seen were D352 and D252. 'V2' No 60915 was observed on a northbound passenger train. D247 (52A) was seen with a Newcastle-Liverpool train (non-stop at York). D349 and D14 were also observed.

Sir Nigel Gresley's original 'V2' design No 60800 *Green Arrow* passed through, light. Likewise, in the opposite direction, did 'A3' 'Pacific' No 60038 *Firdaussi*.

Type 4 D209 (34A) passed straight through with the King's Cross-bound 'Tees-Tyne Pullman'.

'B1' No 61031 *Reedbuck* (50A) brought in a passenger train. Two 'B16s' were observed, Nos 61459 and 61417. Type 4 D14 had a northbound mixed-traffic train. 'V2' No

'A3' No 60038 *Firdaussi*. R. F. Orpwood, the Gresley Society

60908 was seen, light, in the station. 'B1' No 61049 was observed in charge of a northbound passenger train. 'B1' No 61055 passed light through the station.

Type 4 D23 brought in a train from Birmingham. Type 4 D254 (50A) relieved it for the York-Newcastle section. Type 4 D275 had a train of empty coach stock in Platform 8N. 'B16' No 61463 passed through on its way to York sheds.

The Edinburgh-bound 'Talisman' (first stop Newcastle) passed through in the charge of 'A3' No 60080 *Dick Turpin*. At 11.40am the 'Anglo-Scottish Car-Carrier' to the north passed through with D280 on front. Class 'K3' No 61848 passed through the station. A King's Cross-bound passenger train had 'A1' 'Pacific' No 60126 *Sir Vincent Raven* (52B). This was followed by D277 with a train for the same destination. Type 4 D234 headed a northbound Liverpool-Newcastle train. The non-stop northbound 'Elizabethan' came through at 12.40pm in the charge of 'A4' No 60030 *Golden Fleece*. Type 4 diesel D74 passed to the south in charge of a York-Bristol train.

London Midland 'Royal Scot' Class No 46145 *The Royal Artilleryman* (21A) had a northbound passenger train. Class 'A4' 'Pacific' No 60028 *Walter K. Whigham* stopped at York with a Newcastle train. 'B16' No 61476 headed a southbound mixed-traffic train through the station. A three-coach empty train of the passenger brake type passed slowly through the station in the charge of 'A3' No 60051 *Blink Bonny*. At 1.25pm the King's Cross-bound 'Elizabethan' passed through in the charge of Edinburgh 'A4' No 60009 *Union of South Africa*.

The first-stop-Newcastle 'Flying Scotsman' passed through with Type 4 diesel D251. 'Jubilee' Class No 45698 *Mars* was in charge of a northbound passenger train. The southbound first-stop-King's-Cross 'Flying Scotsman' was in the charge of Type 5 'Deltic' D9007 *Pinza*, which is named after the 1953 Derby winner. This follows an LNER tradition of naming locomotives after classic racehorses.

'Britannia' 'Pacific' No 70003 *John Bunyan* gave way to

D275 with a Newcastle train. The 'Britannias' have almost identical whistles to those of the A4s [was this true?]. Class 'A1' No 60146 *Peregrine* passed light through the station. 'B16' No 61847 was in charge of a northbound freight train. Type 4 D351 was observed, as also was D272 (52A) on a

'A1' No 60146 *Peregrine* at Platform 8 of Newcastle Central, heading north on 21 March 1960.

Glasgow train.

'A1' No 60142 *Edward Fletcher* (52B) brought in the King's Cross-bound 'Northumbrian'. It was relieved by an unobtainable 'A1' 'Pacific'. Type 4 D282 had a southbound passenger. D350 was seen heading south with one coach. A southbound King's Cross passenger had 'A4' No 60033 *Seagull*. I noted that its pressure gauge registered 200lb psi.

A southbound parcels train was double-headed by two Midland 4-6-0s, Nos 45263 and 44867. An 'A2' 'Pacific' had a northbound passenger. It was No 60520 *Owen Tudor* (36A). 'A1' No 60140 *Balmoral* made its way to York sheds.

'V2' No 60939 was seen on a southbound freight.

'A4' No 60020 *Guillemot*, seen earlier in the day, was again seen returning to Newcastle. Two locos coupled together, 'V2' Nos 60975 and 65739, headed to York sheds. 'B1' No 61002 *Impala* had a northbound passenger train. Type 4 D252 was observed. Heaton 'A1' 'Pacific' No 60116 *Hal o'the Wynd*, seen earlier, returned on the northbound 'Northumbrian'. 'V2' No 60908 passed south on a parcels

'A4' No 60033 *Seagull*. R. F. Orpwood, the Gresley Society

'A1' No 60140 *Balmoral* comes off the High Level Bridge and enters Gateshead West station on 30 May 1964. *R. F. Orpwood, the Gresley Society*

'V2' No 60939 is also seen at Gateshead West station on the same day. *R. F. Orpwood, the Gresley Society*

train. The northbound 'Heart of Midlothian' was 10 minutes late in the charge of 'A3' No 60054 *Prince of Wales*. Type 4 D280, seen earlier, returned south on the southbound 'Anglo-Scottish Car-Carrier'. D278 was in charge of a southbound passenger. 'V2' No 60960 had a south freight.

At York sheds on my return journey were seen D253, 62039, 62056, 60943, 92143, 60869. 'A2' No 60518 *Tehran* passed us with a southbound passenger train. At Darlington sheds were 'V2' 60905, 90373, 90309, 61198, 62007, 62009, 43102. At Gateshead sheds were 'V2s' 60929 and 60867, D265, 'A4' No 60024 *Kingfisher* and 'A3' No 60080 *Dick Turpin*, which I had observed passing through York on the northbound 'Talisman'. In the Central station, Newcastle, was 'V2' No 60949.

Monday 4 September 1961
Central station, Newcastle-upon-Tyne

'A2' 'Pacific' No 60518 *Tehran* (50A) took over the southbound 'Norseman' from No 67685 (52B). D276 brought in a Birmingham-Newcastle train. D293 brought in a Liverpool-Newcastle train. The northbound 'Anglo-Scottish Car-Carrier' was brought in by D251, which gave way to D260 of the same class.

Type 4 D261 headed in a southbound passenger for King's Cross. It was relieved by 'A4' No 60028 *Walter K. Whigham*. 'A4' No 60022 *Mallard* was in charge of the northbound 'Elizabethan'. D273 had a southbound passenger. D14 brought in the northbound 'Norseman'. No 67683 (52B) relieved it. The southbound 'Queen of Scots' Pullman had D346 on the front. A King's Cross passenger train came in behind 'A4' No 60034 *Lord Farringdon*. 'A4' No 60020 *Guillemot* had the northbound 'Flying Scotsman'. It was relieved by 'A4' No 60016 *Silver King*.

The southbound 'Anglo-Scottish Car-Carrier' was

Opposite: 'A3' No 60080 *Dick Turpin* at Heaton MPD on 29 May 1964.
R. F. Orpwood, the Gresley Society

103

'V2' No 60886 approaches Newcastle Central on 29 May 1964. The 'new' castle keep, which gives the city its name (built 1172-77 by Henry II) is in the left background. *R. F. Orpwood, the Gresley Society*

brought in by 'A3' No 60094 *Colorado* with German-type smoke deflectors. 'V2' No 60806 had a north freight. D293 headed out a Liverpool train. D283 brought in a passenger train from the north. D307 brought in a Liverpool train. D282 was in charge of a southbound parcels.

The 'Heart of Midlothian' to the south was brought in by 'A3' No 60072 *Sunstar* and headed out by 'A4' No 60008 *Dwight D. Eisenhower*. D250 brought in a King's Cross-Glasgow train and D261 took it out.

Tuesday 5 September 1961
'V2' No 60886 was seen with a southbound freight.

'A4' No 60012 *Commonwealth of Australia* had a northbound freight. D353 had the northbound 'North Briton'. The southbound 'Elizabethan' was in the charge of 'A4' No 60022 *Mallard*.

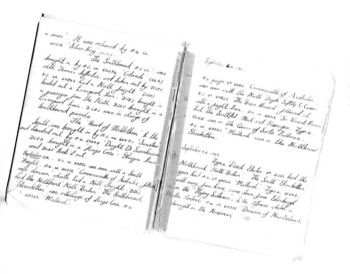

Wednesday 6 September 1961

'A4' 'Pacific' No 60012 *Commonwealth of Australia* was seen with the north 'Anglo-Scottish Car-Carrier'. 'V2' No 60835 *The Green Howard* followed it with a freight train. 'A1' No 60126 *Sir Vincent Raven* had a southbound mail train. D348 was on the 'Queen of Scots' Pullman. 'A4' No 60022 *Mallard* was on the northbound 'Elizabethan'.

Thursday 7 September 1961

Type 4 D351 had the northbound 'North Briton'. The southbound 'Elizabethan' again had 'A4' No 60022 *Mallard*.

Type 4 D209, well away from home, came down from Edinburgh on the 'Flying Scotsman'. In the afternoon, while visiting the Central station, I saw 'A4' No 60013 *Dominion of New Zealand* with the 'Norseman'.

Friday 8 September 1961
Central station, Newcastle-upon-Tyne

Type 4 diesel-electric D276 brought in a passenger train from the south at the same time as 'A3' No 60052 *Prince Palatine* left with the Edinburgh-bound 'Talisman'. Type 4 D248 brought in the northbound 'Anglo-Scottish Car-

'A4' No 60022 *Mallard. R. F. Orpwood, the Gresley Society*

Carrier'. This was given to the charge of 'A4' No 60020 *Guillemot*. 'A1' No 60126 *Sir Vincent Raven* passed south, light, to Gateshead sheds. Type 4 D234 brought in a Liverpool train.

Type 4 D263 brought in a Glasgow-King's Cross passenger, and was relieved by 'A4' No 60006 *Sir Ralph Wedgwood*. 'A4' No 60022 *Mallard* again passed through to the north with the 'Elizabethan'. Type 4 D271 had a mail train and later headed it out to York. Type 4 D345 brought in and took out the 'Queen of Scots' Pullman to the south. Likewise to the north did D277 with the 'Flying Scotsman'. 'A4' No 60033 *Seagull* brought in a King's Cross-Newcastle train immediately preceding it. 'V2' No 60929 was on a northbound cattle train. 'A2' 'Pacific' No 60519 *Honeyway* brought in the southbound 'Anglo-Scottish Car-Carrier' and gave way to D248, returning with the same train. D234 also returned on a Liverpool-bound passenger train.

Monday 11 September 1961
Central station, Newcastle-upon-Tyne

The 'Elizabethan' is off. 'A4' No 60022 *Mallard* was seen going south with the last edition of the train on Saturday 9 September. D114 brought in a Birmingham-Newcastle train. 'A4' No 60029 *Woodcock* brought in the northbound 'Anglo-Scottish Car-Carrier' and 'A3' No 60088 *Book Law* (with German-type smoke deflectors) relieved it. The southbound 'Norseman' was taken out by D284. Type 4 D332 brought in a train from Liverpool. Type 4 D263 brought in a Glasgow-King's Cross train and was relieved by D242. 'B1' No 61032 *Stembok* headed north through the station on a freight train. It was later seen heading in the opposite direction on another freight. 'A2' 'Pacific' No 60538 *Velocity* brought in a Leeds-bound train. 'A3' No 60081 *Shotover* relieved it.

The southbound 'Queen of Scots' Pullman was brought in and taken out by Type 4 D346. 'A4' 'Pacific' No 60026 *Miles Beevor* brought in a train just ahead of the 'Flying

Scotsman' and was relieved by 'A1' No 60147 *North Eastern*. The boat train was brought in by 'A1' 'Pacific' No 60114 *W. P. Allen*. No 67656 took the train forward to the Tyne Commission Quay.

The northbound 'Flying Scotsman' was headed in by D239, which was relieved by 'A3' No 60082 *Neil Gow* (with German-type deflectors). The locomotive moved off without a slip.

The southbound 'Anglo-Scottish Car-Carrier' had 'A4' No 60004 *William Whitelaw*, which was relieved by 'A4' No 60029 *Woodcock* returning home with the same train. Also returning on the same train was D114 seen earlier. Type 4 D253 brought in a train from Colchester. Likewise, from Liverpool, did D309, which ran round immediately to the other end of the train and returned with it later. Unusually, the southbound 'Heart of Midlothian' from Edinburgh had an 'A4' 'Pacific' from King's Cross shed, No 60014 *Silver Link*, which did not uncouple but took water and returned home with the train. From a window on the train one of the

'A3' No 60082 *Neil Gow*. R. F. Orpwood, the Gresley Society

'A4' No 60014 *Silver Link*, the first of the class to be built. *R. F. Orpwood, the Gresley Society*

passengers called out to ask me the name of the locomotive as it was accelerating away.

The 4.14pm King's Cross-Aberdeen train had 'A4' No 60033 *Seagull*, which gave way to 'A2' 'Pacific' No 60529 *Pearl Diver*.

Saturday 16 September 1961
Unusually, 'A4' 'Pacific' No 60003 *Andrew K. McCosh* (34A) was observed at Heaton station on a northbound freight train.

Sunday 17 September 1961
Passing south by Heaton sheds on an Edinburgh-King's Cross train was Type 5 'Deltic' D9003 *Meld*. 'V2' No 60889 was standing on shed almost cold.

Saturday 23 September 1961
Type 5 'Deltic' D9000 was in charge of the northbound

'Flying Scotsman'. 'A4' No 60004 *William Whitelaw* had the southbound 'Queen of Scots' Pullman. 'A2' 'Pacific' No 60538 *Velocity* had a northbound freight. At Heaton sheds later were seen 'A4' No 60004 *William Whitelaw* (turned for a return trip), 'A2' No 60500 *Edward Thompson*, 'A1' No 60147 *North Eastern*, 'A3' No 60073 *St Gatien* (with German-type smoke deflectors), 'V2' No 60922, and Type 4 diesels D286 and D284. A northbound King's Cross-Glasgow train had 'Deltic' D9003 *Meld*. This was immediately followed by a four-coach train in the charge of 'A4' No 60009 *Union of South Africa*.

'A4' No 60009 *Union of South Africa*. R. F. Orpwood, the Gresley Society

Sunday 24 September 1961

Standing in a siding at Heaton sheds was 'A3' No 60089 *Felstead* lowering steam. 'V2' No 60974 was doing the same. 'A2' 'Pacific' No 60500 *Edward Thompson* was standing cold. A diesel shunter towed the cold 'A3' No 60082 *Neil Gow* out of the shed. 'A3' No 60088 *Book Law* was on shed cold. 'A3' No 60085 *Manna* was also seen, as was 'A1'

The crest and 'springbok' plaque carried by No 60009. *Both R. F. Orpwood, the Gresley Society*

No 60151 *Midlothian* and No 60517 *Ocean Swell*. 'V2s' seen were 60944, 60835 *The Green Howard*, *Alexandra, Princess of Wales's Own Yorkshire Regiment* and 60886.

Saturday 30 September 1961
The usual 'Deltic'-hauled 'Flying Scotsman' today had 'A1' No 60147 *North Eastern* (ha!). [This little exclamation obviously registers my delight at diesel being replaced by steam.] 'A1' No 60143 *Sir Walter Scott* passed north immediately afterwards on a passenger train. At Heaton sheds was seen 'A4' No 60024 *Kingfisher*.

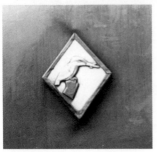

Above and left: The nameplate of 'A4' No 60024 *Kingfisher*, and one of the two bronze enamelled plaques depicting a kingfisher carried by the locomotive. *Both R. F. Orpwood, the Gresley Society*

Opposite: 'A3' No 60040 *Cameronian* at Gateshead on 2 May 1964. *R. F. Orpwood, the Gresley Society*

At Benfield Road was seen 'A1' No 60138 *Boswell*. The last edition of the 'Anglo-Scottish Car-Carrier' had D261. 'Deltic' D9000 had a northbound freight train.

Saturday 14 October 1961

'A3' No 60058 *Blair Athol* had a northbound freight, as also had 'A3' No 60040 *Cameronian*.

Locomotives seen in Heaton sheds were 'A3' Nos 60041 *Salmon Trout*, 60088 *Book Law*, 60096 *Papyrus*, 60082 *Neil Gow* (all with German-type smoke deflectors) and 60037 *Hyperion*, 'A4' 'Pacific' No 60005 *Sir Charles Newton*, 'V2' Nos 60835 *The Green Howard*, *Alexandra, Princess of Wales's Own Yorkshire Regiment*, 60944, 60816, 60805, 'A1' Nos 60154 *Bon Accord*, 60151 *Midlothian*, 60143 *Sir Walter Scott*, 60147 *North Eastern*, 60152 *Holyrood*, 60120 *Kittiwake*, 'A2' Nos 60522 *Straight Deal*, 60526 *Sugar Palm*, and 'B1' No 61305.

'A4' No 60005 *Sir Charles Newton*. R. F. Orpwood, the Gresley Society

In the Central station 'A4' No 60015 *Quicksilver* was seen bringing in a northbound King's Cross-Aberdeen service. Type 5 'Deltic' D9006 had the northbound 'Flying Scotsman'.

Saturday 21 October 1961

In Heaton sheds were seen the following: 'A3' Nos 60037 *Hyperion*, 60085 *Manna*, 60087 *Blenheim* 'V2' Nos 60860 *Durham School*, 60835 *The Green Howard, Alexandra, Princess of Wales's Own Yorkshire Regiment*, 'A4' Nos 60004 *William Whitelaw*, 60002 *Sir Murrough Wilson*, 'A1' No 60137 *Redgauntlet*, 'A2' No 60524 *Herringbone*.

'A3' No 60042 *Singapore* had a northbound freight. 'A3' No 60090 *Grand Parade* passed south on a container train. Type 5 'Deltic' D9000 was on the southbound 'Heart of Midlothian' and 'A3' No 60051 *Blink Bonny* on a northbound King's Cross-Glasgow train.

Thursday 2 November 1961

'A4' No 60026 *Miles Beevor* brought a freight train into Heaton yards and 'A3' No 60090 *Grand Parade* headed it out towards the north. 'A1' No 60155 *Borderer* stood all day in sidings at Heaton Junction on a work train. 'A1' No 60160 *Auld Reekie* had a southbound freight. 'A4' No 60018 *Sparrow Hawk* passed north on a freight. The southbound 'Queen of Scots' Pullman had 'A3' No 60057 *Ormonde*. Type 5 D9010 was on the northbound 'Flying Scotsman'. 'A1' No 60147 *North Eastern* passed through on a southbound passenger train. 'A1' No 60143 *Sir Walter Scott* and 'V2' No 60835 *The Green Howard* were coupled together in Heaton sheds.

Friday 3 November 1961

Type 5 D9000 was on the southbound 'Talisman'. 'A3' No 60099 *Call Boy* had a northbound 'Blue Spot' express fish train. The usual Type 4 on the northbound 'North Briton' was today replaced by 'A1' No 60159 *Bonnie Dundee*. 'A2'

'A3' No 60098 *Spion Kop. R. F. Orpwood, the Gresley Society*

No 60517 *Ocean Swell* headed light southbound. 'A4' No 60018 *Sparrow Hawk* again started north on a freight train. 'A3' No 60098 *Spion Kop* passed north, light.

Saturday 18 November 1961
Heaton 'A2' No 60538 *Velocity* had a northbound parcels train. 'A3' No 60083 *Sir Hugo* was observed returning south light. 'A3' No 60076 *Galopin* was standing in the Quarter-Mile bay. 'A1' No 60132 *Marmion* was seen on a northbound passenger train. 'A3' No 60099 *Call Boy* (with German-type smoke deflectors) stood in the Quarter-Mile bay. 'V2' No 60843 followed No 60538 *Velocity* north with a freight train. Worsdell 'J27' No 65822 headed north with a work train. 'V2' No 60827 passed south on a freight. Type 5 D9000 had the southbound 'Flying Scotsman'.

Saturday 2 December 1961
D9010 observed on the southbound 'Flying Scotsman'.

Saturday 9 December 1961
'A2' No 60511 *Airborne* was seen starting from the Quarter-Mile on a northbound freight.

[This locomotive always had a special significance for me as I was born on the day in 1946 when 'Airborne' won the Derby. Until it was pointed out to him (and, sadly, too late), it had never occurred to my father, a man of the turf, that this would have been the ideal horse on which to place his bet – 'heir born'.]

Sunday 22 December 1961

'Deltic' D9011 was observed on the northbound 'Flying Scotsman'. Passing south on a passenger train was 'A4' No 60012 *Commonwealth of Australia*, back in service after being reportedly stored in bad condition at Carlisle Canal. It looked rather drab even though it had been serviced at Doncaster.

'B1' No 61037 *Jairou* passed north on a parcels semi-fast.

Monday 23 December 1961

'A1' 'Pacific' No 60129 *Guy Mannering* was seen on a northbound express fitted goods van train. Type 4 D257 had a northbound freight, as also did 'A2' 'Pacific' No 60539 *Bronzino*.

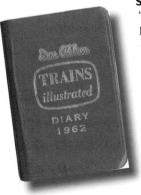

Saturday 6 January 1962

'A3' No 60045 *Lemberg* was seen pulling out from the Quarter-Mile with a northbound freight. 'A1' No 60132 *Marmion* passed north on a passenger. Immediately afterwards came 'A3' No 60099 *Call Boy* on a fast northbound fitted freight. 'A3' No 60076 *Galopin* had a southbound freight. D286 passed south with two vans and a brake van.

My *Trains Illustrated* Diary for 1962.

117

Standing on a somewhat precarious ladder, a fitter gives attention to 'A4' No 60012 *Commonwealth of Australia* in steam at Heaton MPD on 5 June 1963. *R. F. Orpwood, the Gresley Society*

Tuesday 6 March 1962

'A3' 'Pacific' No 60096 *Papyrus* had a northbound freight. 'Deltic' D9013 was in charge of the southbound 'Flying Scotsman'. D275 had the northbound 'North Briton', and D273 passed immediately afterwards on a northbound freight. 'A1' No 60142 *Edward Fletcher* passed south on the 'Queen of Scots' Pullman.

A rare sight: going south on St Peter's Bridge recently was a 'Royal Scot' Class loco, No 46163 *Civil Service Rifleman*, on a passenger train.

[St Peter's Bridge, between Manors and Heaton, carries the East Coast Main Line over the Ouseburn stream at Byker, and runs parallel with the road traffic 'Byker Bridge'.]

Tuesday 20 March 1962

Class 'A4' No 60020 *Guillemot* backed out of the Quarter-Mile, light engine.

Wednesday 21 March 1962

'A3' No 60078 *Night Hawk* was observed heading light on St Peter's Bridge towards Heaton sheds.

Saturday 24 March 1962

Class 'A4' No 60023 *Golden Eagle* headed a short northbound passenger train. 'V2' No 60802 followed with a train of tank wagons. 'A1' 'Pacifics' Nos 60143 *Sir Walter Scott* and 60147 *North Eastern* waited on northbound freights in the Quarter-Mile.

Friday 13 April 1962

Class 'A4' No 60029 *Woodcock* was observed in the Quarter-Mile. It backed away through Heaton Junction. 'A3' No 60045 *Lemberg* headed north on the 'Heart of Midlothian', followed by 'A1' No 60151 *Midlothian* on a freight.

'A3' No 60078 *Night Hawk*. R. F. Orpwood, the Gresley Society

Saturday 14 April 1962

Class 'A3' No 60076 *Galopin* was in charge of the northbound 'Heart of Midlothian'. This was followed immediately by 'A3' No 60071 *Tranquil* on a freight. Class 'B1' No 61242 *Alexander Reith Gray* was seen travelling north light. 'A4' No 60031 *Golden Plover* brought in a train from Scotland and retired to Heaton sheds.

Sunday 15 April 1962

An unusual working was observed in the form of Class 'A4' No 60030 *Golden Fleece* heading 'GUV' and empty coaching stock north of Newcastle from a standstill at Heaton.

(Steam is off the 'Elizabethan'. The 'A4' 'Pacifics' give way to the English Electric Type 5s.)

Good Friday 20 April 1962

All on northbound freight trains from the Quarter-Mile were 'A3' No 60052 *Prince Palatine*, 'A3' No 60078 *Night Hawk* and 'A1' No 60151 *Midlothian*. Class 'A4' No 60023 *Golden Eagle* had a northbound passenger. 'A3' No 60051 *Blink Bonny* was also assigned to a northbound freight.

An example of my *Eagle* boy's diary (1960) used for jotting down loco numbers. Evident here are *Spearmint*, *Sir Vincent Raven*, *Blair Athol*, *Edward Fletcher* and *Sir Hugo*. Among other sportsmen pictured elsewhere in the diary are Henry Cooper, Freddie Trueman and Jimmy Greaves. There is also a photograph of the prototype 'Deltic', with the ominous steam-threatening caption: 'British Railways have ordered 22 Deltics'.

Saturday 21 April 1962

Type 5 D9003 *Meld* was observed on the London-bound 'Flying Scotsman'. Class 'A4' No 60002 *Sir Murrough Wilson* came from Heaton sheds to work a northbound freight from the Quarter-Mile. 'A3' No 60083 *Sir Hugo* worked a northbound passenger train.

Tuesday 24 April 1962
Class 'A2' No 60538 *Velocity* had a northbound passenger train just ahead of the northbound 'Flying Scotsman' in the charge of Type 5 D9016. Type 5 D9019 was observed on the southbound 'Heart of Midlothian'. 'B1' No 61037 *Jairou* was seen going north light.

Friday 27 April 1962
Class 'A2' No 60539 *Bronzino* was observed on a northbound freight. On the northbound 'Heart of Midlothian' was 'A1' No 60147 *North Eastern*.

Friday 4 May 1962
Class 'A4' No 60001 *Sir Ronald Matthews* had a northbound freight from a stand at Heaton. Class 'A2' No 60518 *Tehran* brought in a southbound freight train. The southbound 'Talisman' had Type 5 D9005. 'A3' No 60087 *Blenheim* had the northbound 'Blue Spot' fish. 'A3' No 60076 *Galopin* was observed on a northbound freight from Heaton. 'A4' No 60020 *Guillemot* was seen on St Peter's railway bridge heading a northbound freight. Type 4 D345 had the northbound 'Queen of Scots' Pullman.

Saturday 5 May 1962
Class 'A3' 'Pacific' No 60051 *Blink Bonny* had a northbound freight, as also did 'A3' No 60076 *Galopin*. 'A3' No 60053 *Sansovino* headed light south. 'A1' No 60132 *Marmion* had the northbound 'Blue Spot' fish. 'V2' No 60833 was also observed.

Modified 'A4' allocations: Nos 60031 *Golden Plover* and 60027 *Merlin* to 65B (St Rollox).

Age 16
1962-63

Monday 2 July 1962

Class 'A3' No 60083 *Sir Hugo* was observed starting south from Heaton sheds.

Tuesday 3 July 1962

Diesel-electric D5086 was seen on a short northbound passenger train. The northbound 'Heart of Midlothian' had 'Deltic' D9000 *Royal Scots Grey*. Type 4 D346 was seen on the southbound 'North Briton' at approx 7.15pm.

Two strange steam 'Pacific' workings were observed: strange because of reports that the locomotives were in store and about to be scrapped. The first concerns 'A3' No 60099 *Call Boy*, which was in store at St Margarets (64A) Edinburgh.

'A3' No 60099 *Call Boy*. R. F. Orpwood, the Gresley Society

This was seen on a southbound fish train at approx 7.00pm. The 'Pacific' itself was travelling at a good 40mph and did not appear too much the worse for wear. In mid-March it had been joined in its stored condition by Class 'A1' 'Pacific' No 60160 *Auld Reekie* of Haymarket shed.. The second case was also of another 'A3' 'Pacific' in the form of No 60101 *Cicero* of Haymarket (64B), which was observed heading north with a brake van. Cicero did not have German-type smoke deflectors and was in store at Galashiels in mid-March. Both *Cicero* and No 60100 *Spearmint* were reported 'dead'. My observation of *Cicero* leads me to believe that *Spearmint* has also been reprieved, at least for the time being. [In fact, I observed No 60100 on Saturday 2 March 1963.]

Finally, an unusual working involved a Type 4 diesel and a 'V2' travelling south together at a considerable rate through Heaton yards.

Much widespread scrapping of steam is now taking place. In the ER especially, the Gresley 'V2s' and 'A3' Class locomotives are gradually being withdrawn. Of the 'V2s' to go are Nos 60850, 60875, 60928, 60960, 60977, 60826, 60849, 60917, 60811, 60823, 60857, 60867. Confirmed 'A3' withdrawals are Nos 60035 *Windsor Lad*, 60055 *Woolwinder*, 60064 *Tagalie*, 60079 *Bayardo*, 60093 *Coronach*, 60095 *Flamingo*, 60105 *Solario*.

20 of these 'Pacifics' will be withdrawn in 1962.

Three of Haymarket's Class 'A4' 'Pacifics' have been removed to other sheds. These are Nos 60027 *Merlin*, 60031 *Golden Plover* and 60009 *Union of South Africa*. The former two are at St Rollox in order to work 3-hour summer trains between Glasgow and Aberdeen. No 60009 has been moved to Ferryhill (61B) Aberdeen, and it is believed to be also sharing this task.

On 18 June 1962 the production 'Deltic' Type 5s entered service on the new summer timetable. This day [the day I remember on which I sat for my first O level examination] also happened to be the centenary of 'The Flying Scotsman', which was acknowledged with ceremony at both terminals as well as at Newcastle.

Haymarket has named its first two 'Deltics' D9000 *Royal Scots Grey* and D9010 *The King's Own Scottish Borderer*. The 'Elizabethan' is again in service with a 'Deltic' in charge. As yet I haven't witnessed this train. The summer 'Anglo-Scottish Car-Carrier' is also running again. It has been observed by myself in the charge of an 'A4' 'Pacific' and a Type 4. Type 5 'Deltic' D9007 *Pinza* was recently seen on the 'Talisman' heading north of Newcastle, leading me to understand that these trains now make runs between the capitals without a change of engine.

Monday 9 July 1962
Class 'A1' 'Pacific' No 60155 *Borderer* headed out north with a freight from the Quarter-Mile. 'V2' No 60947 was observed hurtling south on a fast mixed freight.

Wednesday 11 July 1962
Class 'A2' 'Pacific' No 60538 *Velocity* of Heaton shed picked up a freight and headed north. It was soon followed, heading another freight, by 'A3' 'Pacific' No 60037 *Hyperion*, looking in good condition. A 'V2' headed into Newcastle with the evening 'Blue Spot' fish. Its number was unclear, being either 60922 or 60942. After quite a pause in my observations of workings, 'Deltic' D9013 headed an Edinburgh-bound passenger. It was followed by 'A3' No 60076 *Galopin* with a brake van. Steam traction is seldom seen on the Anglo-Scottish passenger services these days. On 9 June the whistle of an 'A4' 'Pacific' was heard on a southbound passenger, and an 'A4' was also recently observed on both the 'Queen of Scots' Pullman and the 'Anglo-Scottish Car-Carrier'. But this is now the exception rather than the rule. Type 4 D348 had the southbound 'North Briton'. An unidentifiable 'A4' 'Pacific' was observed during the morning at Manors.

'A3' No 60037 *Hyperion*. R. F. Orpwood, the Gresley Society

Thursday 12 July 1962

An unidentifiable 'A4' seen from a distance was observed travelling slowly south on a long freight train. 'Deltic' D9016 was seen on a northbound passenger. D5108 headed a southbound freight. This locomotive appears to be a regular on this particular train at approximately 6.50pm each evening. The usual 'Blue Spot' fish had 'A1' No 60151 *Midlothian* instead of the regular 'V2'.

'V2' No 60860 *Durham School* had a northbound freight. D239 headed south on a freight. 'A2' No 60521 *Watling Street* was next observed on a southbound four-vehicle train that consisted of three passenger brake vans and a horse box. 'A2' No 60538 *Velocity* again had a northbound freight from a stand in the Quarter-Mile. Finally, an 'A2' 'Pacific' was observed awaiting the road from the Quarter-Mile on a northbound freight. It was No 60511 *Airborne*.

Friday 20 July 1962

A Type 4 diesel had the southbound 'North Briton'. D358 also had a train of vans in the same direction. D355 was seen waiting to pick up a freight from the Quarter-Mile. 'Deltic' D9017 had a King's Cross-Edinburgh train at approx 8.15pm. The only large steam locomotive seen was 'A3' No 60098 *Spion Kop*, which was not equipped with German-type smoke deflectors. It headed a northbound freight from the Quarter-Mile. Seldom are steam locomotives now seen on express passenger trains in the Heaton area.

Monday 23 July 1962

Type 4 diesels now seemingly appear to be in charge of just about every train that passes. This is a great pity because not only are the Type 4s a particularly characterless class, but also a monotonous colour. At least the 'Deltics' have some hint of colour [referring here to the earliest days when their livery was a two-tone green]. D348 was observed on the southbound 'North Briton'. D272 had a southbound freight. Three steam locomotives were seen, however. 'A3'

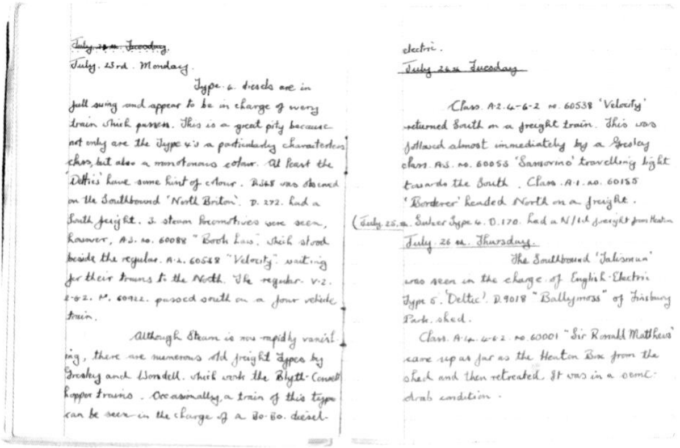

127

No 60088 *Book Law* stood parallel to No 60538 *Velocity* waiting with their freights to the north. 'V2' No 60922 passed to the south with a four-vehicle train.

Although steam is now rapidly vanishing, there are numerous old freight types, eg 'J' Class and 'Q' Class, which work the Blyth-Consett hopper trains, but even these trains are often to be seen in the charge of Bo-Bo diesels.

Tuesday 24 July 1962

'A2' No 60538 *Velocity* returned south with a freight train. This was followed almost immediately by 'A3' No 60053 *Sansovino* travelling light to the south. 'A1' No 60155 *Borderer* headed north on a freight.

Thursday 26 July 1962

The southbound 'Talisman' was seen in the charge of 'Deltic' D9018 *Ballymoss* of Finsbury Park shed. Class 'A4' No 60001 *Sir Ronald Matthews* came up as far as Heaton box from the sheds, and then retreated. It was in a semi-drab condition.

Friday 27 July 1962

The southbound 'Flying Scotsman' was observed on time in the charge of Finsbury Park Type 5 D9015 *Tulyar*. I observed the northbound 'Elizabethan' at approx 1.45pm (about 15 minutes earlier than in previous years) in the charge of Type 5 D9012 *Crepello*. A mail train passed south with Type 4 D272, and this was followed by the southbound 'Anglo-Scottish Car-Carrier' with D384. This train now uses 'Eastern Region Car Transporters' instead of the older single-deck vehicles of previous years.

The 'Elizabethan' service, which runs only during the summer months, has at last broken its non-stop world record of over 390 miles. It has been forced to pause at Newcastle Central in order to make a crew change. The southern crews are reported to have agreed to ride for over 6 hours on the 'Deltic' engines now concerned, but their northern colleagues would not agree. So the world non-stop record passes to France, to the now unchallenged 'Sud Express' (Paris-Bordeaux, 359.8 miles non-stop).

The 'Elizabethan' was taken off completely in the summer schedule of 1963 as the BTC (British Transport Commission) considered that the 'Flying Scotsman' had enough prestige with the public. The former 'Elizabethan' still runs about 10 mins behind the 'Flying Scotsman' each summer weekday, but in a nameless form.

Saturday 28 July 1962

An 'A4' 'Pacific' was observed on a northbound passenger train, but it was unidentifiable being at a distance. D169 had a northbound passenger and D348 the northbound 'North Briton'. Class 'A1' 60162 *Saint Johnstoun* passed south on a passenger train. 'V2' No 60860 *Durham School* (52B) arrived into Heaton yards to work a northbound freight.

Monday 30 July 1962

The southbound 'Anglo-Scottish Car-Carrier' had Type 4 D257. This was followed by the southbound 'Queen of Scots' Pullman with 'Deltic' D9007 *Pinza* of Finsbury Park in charge. Again in charge of the northbound 'Elizabethan' (now no longer non-stop) was D9012 *Crepello*. Later, in the evening, 'A4' No 60018 *Sparrow Hawk* headed a 'Blue Spot' north. It was preceded by 'V2' No 60833 on a northbound freight.

'A4' No 60018 *Sparrow Hawk*. R. F. Orpwood, the Gresley Society

Tuesday 31 July 1962

The southbound 'Queen of Scots' Pullman was observed with a Class 'A2' 'Pacific' No 60538 *Velocity*. Type 5 D9003 *Meld* headed north on the 'Flying Scotsman', a good hour ahead of its 1961 time. A few minutes later, the 'Elizabethan' followed with D9008 of Gateshead shed. Thus it appears that the 'Deltics' from any of their allocated sheds are being used to work this train, which was never worked by a Gateshead 'A4'.

Wednesday 1 August 1962

An 'A4' 'Pacific' was observed heading north at Benton Bank on the longest freight I have yet seen. It was composed of vans and passenger brakes.

Sunday 5 August 1962

'A2' No 60517 *Ocean Swell* headed a northbound freight from Heaton yards behind Class 'V2' No 60933, also on a northbound freight.

Observations from a train journey Newcastle-Darlington-Newcastle, Wednesday 8 August 1962

On the outward journey the diesel railcar set used the north platform of the station and took the diamond crossing onto the High Level Bridge. 'Deltic' D9004 was bringing in the southbound 'Talisman', passing 'A3' No 60071 *Tranquil* as it brought to a halt a northbound passenger. This locomotive was giving way to 'A2' No 60530 *Sayajirao*, which was observed reversing into the station over the diamond crossing as our diesel railcar set headed out. At Gateshead sheds three 'A4' 'Pacifics' were standing in line: Nos 60023 *Golden Eagle*, 60019 *Bittern* and, between them, 60025 *Falcon*.

'A3' No 60041 *Salmon Trout* and Type 5 D9018 *Ballymoss* were also observed.

Opposite: 'A3' No 60071 *Tranquil* at Heaton MPD on 2 May 1964.
R. F. Orpwood, the Gresley Society

'A4' No 60025 *Falcon*. R. F. Orpwood, the Gresley Society

As the train headed south, 'A3' No 60085 *Manna* passed in the opposite direction on a freight. At Darlington were seen 'V2' Nos 60879 and 60954, the latter on a northbound passenger train. A named Type 4 D235 *Apapa* had a northbound passenger train. 2-6-0 No 43129 was observed at Darlington shed, as also were No 69006 and 'V2' No 60915. The 'Flying Scotsman' passed outside Darlington station at speed with a 'Deltic' in charge, and the 'Elizabethan' passed our train at very great speed to the north. On the return journey 'V2' No 60809 *The Snapper, The East Yorkshire Regiment, The Duke of York's Own* was observed in Darlington station. D47 had a southbound mail train. The train back to Newcastle was fast, behind Type 4 D349.

Durham, Tuesday 14 August 1962
Crossing the Durham Viaduct on its way to Newcastle with a passenger train was 'A4' No 60013 *Dominion of New Zealand*. Heading south on the viaduct was 'Deltic' D9003 *Meld* with a Pullman train.

York station, Friday 17 August 1962

The outward-bound train from Newcastle was a diesel railcar set. It made reasonably good time with no exceptionally high speeds. The unit stopped at Chester le Street, Durham, Ferryhill, Darlington, Northallerton, Thirsk and finally York. From the train numerous locomotives were observed, including Class 'A4' 'Pacific' No 60001 *Sir Ronald Matthews* on a northbound freight. While the train was at a standstill at Thirsk, 'Deltic' D9005 headed south through the station at tremendous speed on an Edinburgh-King's Cross train. 'A3' No 60075 *St Frusquin* was seen on shed at York, as was 'A3' No 60110 *Robert the Devil*. This later went south light through the station. Class 'A1' No 60138 *Boswell* had a northbound passenger. Another Class 'A1' No 60154 *Bon Accord* brought in a parcels and made for the shed. 'Deltic' D9006 brought in a King's Cross-bound train and, while awaiting departure, was passed by 'Deltic' D9001 *St Paddy* on the northbound 'Talisman', which took the express track through the station.

Class 'A1' 'Pacific' No 60147 *North Eastern* of Heaton shed brought in a southbound passenger, and was relieved by 'V2' No 60871. *North Eastern* was observed later in the day on a northbound train. 'A1' No 60146 *Peregrine* stood with steam up all day on Platform 8S and finally backed down to York motive power depot. Class 'V2' No 60954 was seen on a northbound freight, as was again observed on southbound wagons. 'A3' No 60068 *Sir Visto* passed south through the station light. The southbound 'Tees-Tyne Pullman' had D166, which made a short stop of about 3 minutes. 'V2' No 60939 took a train of empty coaching stock south.

Named Type 4 D215 *Aquitania* brought in a Newcastle-Liverpool train. 'Deltic' D9009 *Alycidon* had the southbound 'Flying Scotsman'. 'Deltic' D9010 (which should have the nameplates *The King's Own Scottish Borderer* but didn't) had charge of the southbound 'Elizabethan'. The northbound 'Elizabethan' had 'Deltic' D9018 *Ballymoss*.

'A3' No 60075 St Frusquin at Heaton MPD on 2 May 1964. R. F. Orpwood, the Gresley Society

The northbound 'Flying Scotsman' had 'Deltic' D9015 *Tulyar*. The southbound 'Talisman' had 'Deltic' D9014, and 'Deltic' D9000 *Royal Scots Grey* had a southbound passenger [the age of the 'Deltics' had truly arrived].

Type 4 D271 had the southbound 'Anglo-Scottish Car-Carrier'. D174 had the northbound version of this train. Class 'B1' No 61027 *Madoqua* passed south light through the station. 'B1' No 61138 coupled to an A1A-A1A diesel headed south on a passenger. They later came back north on a passenger. Co-Co Type 3 diesel D6770 passed south through the station, freshly painted in a high gloss, with even the buffers silvered and unsullied. 2-6-0 No 43097 passed north light. 'V2' No 60749 headed a northbound passenger. 'Britannia' Class 7 No 70012 *John of Gaunt* headed for York MPD. Type 4 D243 headed a Liverpool-bound train. A northbound passenger was observed in the charge of Class 'B1' No 61017 *Bushbuck*. Class 'V2' No 60803 headed a first-stop-Newcastle train out of York. 'A1' 'Pacific' No 60149 *Amadis* brought in a northbound passenger. Another northbound passenger had 'A3' No 60103 *Flying Scotsman*, which made a stop at York. 'A1' No 60153 *Flamboyant* took a freight train south.

The return journey was made on the 'Northumbrian' with D278 of York MPD. Departure was at approx 4.40pm. Arrival at Newcastle Central approx 6.15pm. Stops were made at Darlington and Durham. Locomotives seen on the return journey were 'A2' No 60526 *Sugar Palm* at York MPD, 'B1' No 61032 *Stembok* at Ferryhill, 'B1' No 61037 *Jairou* on a southbound freight, and at Darlington shed 'V2' No 60809 *The Snapper, The East Yorkshire Regiment, The Duke of York's Own*.

Tuesday 21 August 1962
'A4' No 60014 *Silver Link* was observed in the Heaton area.

Saturday 1 September 1962
'Deltic' D9020 *Nimbus* observed on a northbound passenger train.

Tuesday 4 September 1962
Carlisle Citadel station

'Coronation' 'Pacific' No 46242 *City of Glasgow* in green livery was observed on the 11.00am northbound passenger from Carlisle. Heading light through the station was 'Princess' 'Pacific' No 46200 *The Princess Royal*. The

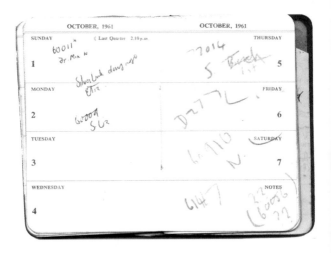

Another example of the notebooks/diaries I used on the spot. The left-hand page makes reference to 'A4' No 60011 on a northbound mixed freight, 'A4' *Silver Link* on the 'Elizabethan' and 'A4' No 60009 on the southbound 'Elizabethan' ('S. Liz').

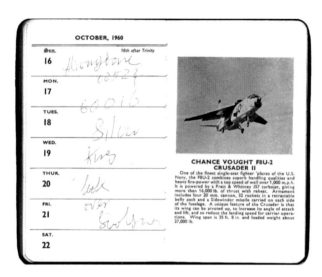

Sun. 16	18th after Trinity
MON. 17	
TUES. 18	
WED. 19	
THUR. 20	
FRI. 21	
SAT. 22	

CHANCE VOUGHT F8U-2 CRUSADER II

One of the finest single-seat fighter 'planes of the U.S. Navy, the F8U-2 combines superb handling qualities and heavy fire-power with a top speed of well over 1,000 m.p.h. It is powered by a Pratt & Whitney J57 turbojet, giving more than 16,000 lb. of thrust with reheat. Armament includes four 20 mm. cannon, 32 rockets in a retractable belly pack and a Sidewinder missile carried on each side of the fuselage. A unique feature of the Crusader is that its wing can be pivoted up, to increase its angle of attack and lift, and so reduce the landing speed for carrier operations. Wing span is 35 ft. 8 in. and loaded weight about 27,000 lb.

This page records 'A4' No 60016 *Silver King* taking over the Edinburgh-bound 'Flying Scotsman' at Newcastle. See the entry for 21 March 1960, and accompanying photograph.

doyen of the class. It was in red livery and recently shared in the hauling of the 'Aberdeen Flyer' enthusiasts' special on its West Coast return route. The southbound 'Royal Scot' had Type 4 D323. This was followed immediately by the southbound 'Thames-Clyde' in the charge of D157. A Birmingham-bound passenger train was noted in the charge of Type 4 D300.

'Coronation' No 46233 *Duchess of Sutherland* (green livery) worked an Edinburgh-bound passenger. The southbound 'Waverley' had Type 4 D98. 'Jubilee' No 45686 *St Vincent* headed light towards the south through the station. D30 had a northbound passenger. Also heading light towards the south went 'Royal Scot' No 46141 *The*

North Staffordshire Regiment. The northbound 'Royal Scot' had D379, and the southbound 'Mid-Day Scot' had D290. A Type 4 diesel brought in a train and gave way to 'Royal Scot' No 46118 *Royal Welch Fusilier* to continue its journey north. A southbound passenger came in, its Type 4 giving way to 'Coronation' No 46234 *Duchess of Abercorn* (green livery).

Wednesday 5 September 1962

'A4' No 60001 *Sir Ronald Matthews* was seen going north on a freight from the yard at Heaton.

The Southbound 'Waverley' had Sulzer Type 4 D18. 'Jubilee' 45466 'St Vincent' headed light towards the South through the station. Sulzer D30 had a Northbound passenger. Also heading light towards the South next. 'Royal Scot' No 46161 'The North Staffordshire Regiment'. The Northbound 'Royal Scot' had D379, and the Southbound 'Mid-day Scot' had D290. A Type 4 diesel brought in a train and gave way to 'Royal Scot' No 46118 'Royal Welch Fusilier' to continue on its journey North. A Southbound passenger came in, its Type 4 giving way to 'Coronation' 46234 'Duchess of Abercorn'. (Seen.)

September 5th: 'A4'
Class A4 No 60001 'Sir Ronald Matthews' was seen going North on a freight from the yard at Heaton.

September 8th
Class A4 No 60001 (5xx) 'Sir Ronald Matthews' again had a Northbound freight train from Heaton. Class A2 pacific No 60519 'Honeyway' was seen setting the pace on a Northbound passenger. V2 No 60940 had a South mixed. and V2 60900 had a N/bd freight in the wake of 60001. Deltic D9011 had the N/bd 'Flying Scotsman'. (A1 pacific 60123 'H.A. Ivatt' was completely wrecked in a freight train collision at Offord. in which 50 wagons were derailed.) (Sep 8th 1962) This derailment caused D9011 to be 2 hours late on the 'Flying Scotsman'.

September 11th
An A4 pacific was observed in charge of the Southbound 'Queen of Scots' Pullman during the afternoon (8th). D9007 'Pinza' had the S/bd 'Heart of Midlothian'.

Saturday 8 September 1962

'A4' No 60001 *Sir Ronald Matthews* again had a northbound freight train from Heaton. 'A2' No 60519 *Honeyway* was seen setting the pace on a northbound passenger train. 'V2' No 60940 had a southbound mixed traffic. 'V2' No 60900 had a northbound freight in the wake of No 60001. 'Deltic' D9011 had the northbound 'Flying Scotsman'.

'A1' No 60123 *H. A. Ivatt* was completely wrecked in a freight train collision at Offord yesterday in which 50 wagons were derailed. The derailment apparently caused D9011 to be 2 hours late with the 'Flying Scotsman'.

Tuesday 11 September 1962
An unobtainable 'A4' 'Pacific' was observed in charge of the southbound 'Queen of Scots' Pullman during the afternoon (*?!). [The exclamatory brackets must have been my indication of the now comparative rarity of such a working.]

D9007 *Pinza* had the southbound 'Heart of Midlothian'.

Wednesday 27 February 1963
An unidentifiable 'V2' observed heading south at Benton Bank. 'A3' No 60041 *Salmon Trout* headed a northbound freight at the same spot as also No 60087 *Blenheim* with a southbound freight.

'A3' No 60041 *Salmon Trout* climbs Benton Bank north of Heaton Junction with a freight on 27 February 1963.

Above: 'A3' No 60087 *Blenheim* heads south on Benton Bank towards Heaton Junction with a southbound freight on 2 March 1963.

Saturday 2 March 1963

'A2' No 60525 *A. H. Peppercorn* was seen climbing Benton Bank with a northbound passenger train. 'V2' No 60865 had a northbound freight here as did 'A4' *Sir Ronald Matthews* and 'A3' No 60051 *Blink Bonny* and 'A3' No 60100 *Spearmint* a southbound freight. 'Deltic' D9007 *Pinza* headed a northbound passenger train.

Sunday 3 March 1963

'Deltic' D9007 *Pinza* returned with a southbound passenger train.

Main picture: No 60525 A. H. Peppercorn climbs Benton Bank by the W. D. & H. O. Wills tobacco factory on the A1058 Coast Road, Heaton, on 2 March 1963.

Main picture: 'A4' No 60001 *Sir Ronald Matthews* climbs Benton Bank with a train of wagons on the same day.

Below: Also on 2 March 1963 'A3' No 60051 *Blink Bonny* climbs north out of Heaton past the double-arm semaphore signal on Benton Bank.

Below: 'A3' No 60100 *Spearmint* descends Benton Bank towards Heaton on that Saturday.

'Deltic' D9007 *Pinza* climbs Benton Bank past the Wills factory on 2 March 1963.

'Deltic' D9007 *Pinza* returns on the following day, 3 March 1963, photographed at the same spot.

Ages 17-19
1963-65

Wednesday 21 August 1963
Carlisle Citadel station

Main-line Class 1 workings of named and other trains of primary importance were found to be mainly diesel-hauled by English Electric Type 4 and Sulzer Type 4 locomotives. The southbound 'Waverley' was in the charge of D18. This train was stationary on the platform for about 10 minutes, while a second southbound passenger brought in by D374 received 'Royal Scot' No 46141 *The North Staffordshire Regiment* as relief engine.

Stanier 'Pacific' No 46249 *City of Sheffield* headed a four-coach train north from Carlisle. The southbound 'Royal Scot' had D302, which stopped for 2 minutes. Type 4 D98 had the southbound 'Thames-Clyde'. Class 5MT 4-6-0

'A4' No 60026 *Miles Beevor. R. F. Orpwood, the Gresley Society*

No 73121 headed in a passenger train from the north, which terminated at Carlisle.

Type 4 D379 had a northbound passenger, while a freight train on a parallel track awaited the right of way in the charge of 'Jubilee' No 45629 *Straits Settlements*. Two other locomotives of interest observed were 'Royal Scot' Nos 46110 *Grenadier Guardsman* and 46168 *The Girl Guide*.

Thursday 22 August 1963
Newcastle Central station

Newcastle Central Station was found to be even more dieselised than Carlisle. Among the total number of locomotives observed, only three were steam engines, two of these being 'Pacifics' and the other a 'B1' 4-6-0. One of these 'Pacifics' was an unidentifiable 'A3'. The other was 'A4' No 60026 *Miles Beevor* observed on its way to Gateshead sheds.

The 'B1' was No 61216, which had brought in a train of coaching stock from Sunderland. All Class 1 trains from the south were diesel-hauled. D9010 had the northbound 'Flying Scotsman'. One of the recently introduced Brush Type 4s D1530 had the northbound boat train, and the prototype diesel-electric DP2 was on the former 'Elizabethan'.

[I travelled from King's Cross to Newcastle behind DP2 only two weeks before it was completely destroyed in a collision on 31 July 1967. My personal diary entry for 14 July reads: 'Took the 12.00pm train from King's Cross arriving into Newcastle at 4.40pm – 25 minutes late – behind experimental locomotive DP2.' The entry for Tuesday 1 August reads: 'This morning's post was much delayed because of a big passenger train accident at Thirsk yesterday. The 12.00pm King's Cross-Edinburgh (our train of 14 July) hit a derailed cement train at 50mph – 7 killed and 40 badly hurt.' The entry for 11 August reads: 'It is interesting to note that the 12.00pm Edinburgh train wrecked a few days ago causing 7 deaths and numerous injuries when colliding with a derailed freight train, was not only our train of 14 July but also had the same diesel-electric DP2, which seemed on some television shots tonight to have been completely devastated.']

From the north the contingent was as follows: Brush Type 4 D1523 on the 'Anglo-Scottish Car-Carrier', Type 4 D170 on the 'Queen of Scots' Pullman, and Type 5 D9018 *Ballymoss* on the 'Heart of Midlothian'.

It may be well to mention here that diesel traction is now almost predominant at Newcastle for a number of reasons. From the beginning of the summer schedule, steam was banished completely from the Great Northern main line south of Peterborough. All Class 1 workings from King's Cross are now rostered to Finsbury Park 'Deltic' units, Brush and Sulzer Type 4 diesels. From 17 June Heaton shed, a sub-depot of Gateshead, which in steam days used to share Gateshead's steam rosterings, was closed to all steam traction. Gateshead and Heaton, King's Cross and Haymarket now no longer have any regular steam-hauled Class 1 workings. In spite of this, however, steam engines are still to be found at Heaton and are sometimes in evidence on passenger trains into Newcastle from Scotland. On Saturday 24 August Class 'A3' No 60060 *The Tetrarch*... [page missing]

Tuesday 3 September 1963
Observed heading north on a passenger train at approximately 2.05pm was Type 5 D9013 *The Black Watch*. This was followed by a 'V2' on a northbound passenger train.

Thursday 5 September 1963
'V2' No 60868 was observed on a northbound four-coach passenger train, and this was followed by Peterborough-allocated 'A4' No 60007 *Sir Nigel Gresley* on a northbound freight at Benton Bank.

In the opposite direction a container train had Type 4 D399.

'A4' No 60007 *Sir Nigel Gresley. R. F. Orpwood, the Gresley Society*

Saturday 7 September 1963
Observed an unidentifiable 'A4' on a heavy southbound passenger train at approx 1.35pm.

Age 18
1964

August 1964
Recent observations have been of Class 'A3' 'Pacific' No 60112 *St Simon* on Pilgrim Street bridge just north of Newcastle Central, and of 'B1' No 61226 *Sassaby* on a short freight train on consecutive days at Pelaw. 'A3' No 60070 *Gladiateur* on a condemned dump at Heaton shed.

Saturday 24 October 1964
Observe the late arrival of the advertised 'Jubilee Requiem' train from King's Cross to Newcastle at the Central station behind 'A4' No 60009 *Union of South Africa*.

THE LAST 'STREAK' STEAMS IN . . . LATE

THE last "streak" to haul a passenger train into Newcastle Central Station steamed majestically to a stop today — 37 minutes late.

It was 60009, class A.4 "Union of South Africa," pulling an excursion train carrying members of the Stephenson Locomotive Society from King's Cross to Newcastle.

SENTIMENTAL

It will be the last engine of its type—they include the world steam record-holder "Mallard" — to bring a passenger train into the station.

Most of the once proud "streaks"—the nickname for the streamlined Pacifics—have now been relegated to hauling goods trains. One is in Gateshead depot.

For many of the passengers today's was a purely sentimental journey.

One member of the society, 21-year-old Mr. R. A. Copeland, of Brookman's Park, Hertfordshire, said: "I think I'm sad to see the end of these locomotives. I'm a great admirer of the Gresley Pacifics."

The driver, Mr. Robert Lummiss, of London, said: "I suppose I have a few regrets but you really can't beat diesel trains for power."

The delay in the arrival of the "Jubilee Requiem"—the name was carried on a special plate on the front of the locomotive—was due to a broken rail near Doncaster.

A number of other trains from the South were also held up.

Extract from the *Newcastle Evening Chronicle*.

Age 19
1965

Saturday 18 September 1965
'A4' chime whistle heard at Heaton Junction.

AFTERWORD
1966-68

At this point my railway diary ends. However, in the personal journal that I kept (and continue to keep) throughout succeeding years I interspersed sporadic observations of steam workings until their end in 1968. Old habits die hard, and for the sake of completion I've included them here.

British Rail Inter-City 125 power car No 43095 *Heaton* at King's Cross in the early 1980s.

Sunday 9 January 1966
Cycled down to the Coast Road railway bridge. Saw D9020 *Nimbus* on a southbound passenger train. Cycled home as it was rather cold.

Wednesday 30 March 1966
[A somewhat prophetic diary entry on this day reads:] I saw a southbound train of mineral wagons at the Quarter-Mile headed by 'K1' 2-6-0 No 62027. Very refreshing and brings back happy memories of the former glory that was steam. I am determined to write a recollective essay on it some time.

Wednesday 13 July 1966
[On this day I set off on a summer visit to a former school friend in Clitheroe, Lancashire.]

The Carlisle train left Newcastle Central at 6.45am and it was a stopping one. Therefore it didn't get in until around 8.35 or so. The Preston train didn't leave until 10.23, so I had to hang around at Carlisle, still a comparative stronghold of the steam engine. I noticed a lot of station pilots, a Stanier 4-6-0, and also one 'Britannia' 'Pacific', No 70018, formerly *Flying Dutchman* but minus nameplates, although the name had been painted back on. It was grimy, a shadow of former days. Also saw 'Britannia' No 70028 (formerly *Royal Star*). The run from Carlisle to Preston was fast, headed by a Brush Sulzer diesel through Penrith, down Shap through thick mist and rain, through Tebay, Oxenholme, Lancaster and into Preston.

Thursday 14 July 1966
Clitheroe seems to be one of the last strongholds of steam in England. It has a little station, but the trains are big and go to Skipton, and can be diverted this way from the LM main line. Also, there is a branch line for a cement works. The whole system here is exclusively steam-operated. I have noticed two Stanier 4-6-0s and an Ivatt, and also what seemed to be a 'Britannia' heading a very fast goods – or was it a 9F? [Obviously a distant view.]

Friday 15 July 1966
It poured with rain best part of today. A 'Britannia' 'Pacific' (?) took a fast passenger train through here at about 75mph at 1.00am or so.

Tuesday 19 July 1966
[This was the summer of England's victory in the World Cup and my school friend and I had somehow managed to obtain tickets for the match between Brazil (Pelé) and Portugal (Eusebio) at Goodison Park.]

Left the station at Clitheroe in a coach at about 5.15pm where there was a Stanier 2-8-0 8F No 48165. The coach skirted Preston and went down the M6 motorway to Everton's ground (Goodison Park). Arrived there at about 7.05 and there was a Scots Guards band playing. My first football match. A tremendous atmosphere and quite novel to me. What strikes you most of all is the colour of the grass and the football jerseys [this was written in the days before colour TV]. The teams were Brazil and Portugal and the latter won 3-1 after the most famous footballer in the world, Pelé of Brazil, had been injured. It was a great thrill seeing this man personally.

Wednesday 27 July 1966
Got into Preston at about 2.45pm and went straight to the station. I caught a fleeting glimpse of a 'Britannia' 'Pacific' on a southbound passenger train. There is still quite a lot of steam traction on the LMR. My train left at 3.22 and had a Brush diesel D1622, which made excellent time until Shap, where it was held up and had to restart on the crippling incline, achieving therefore only about 30mph until Shap Summit. The train was about 7 minutes late into Carlisle, where I saw 'Britannia' 'Pacific' No 70012 *John of Gaunt*, and the Newcastle train left at 5.35, arriving at 7.15. Newcastle to Carlisle is a beautiful line, but steam is now absolutely extinct there.

Saturday 27 August 1966
This morning a BR Standard Class 5 hurtled north, light engine, from Heaton at speed. I estimate 70mph. It was shortly followed by a procession of three steam freight locomotives [I don't record the classes] coupled together.

Saturday 3 September 1966
I had occasion to cycle along Marleen Avenue and was surprised to see several steam locomotives in the vicinity of Heaton shed, including a 9F.

Tuesday 13 September 1966
I was right on the scene this evening at Benfield Road when a BR Standard 2-6-0 went north at about 45mph with a shortish train of hopper and mineral wagons. This is a remarkable occurrence at Heaton – and indeed on the whole East Coast these days. It was phenomenal luck to be in the vicinity. I waited when I heard the distant approach of a train and, as it got nearer, I could have sworn it was making the type of approach a fast steam loco used to make. I was quite prepared for a diesel. Nevertheless, it soon revealed itself as the above-mentioned. The glare from its fire was visible in the steam.

Sunday 2 October 1966
[On this day I joined the 'Wansbeck Piper' – the final steam-hauled passenger train to travel on the old North British line (known locally as 'The Wannie') from Morpeth to Woodburn in Northumberland. It also happened to coincide with the last day of the trolleybus system in Newcastle, and on the previous day I had made a point of taking my last ride on trolleybus NBB 611.]

The train, the 'Wansbeck Piper', was 11 coaches pulled by two Ivatt 2-6-0s, Nos 43000 and 43063. It was piped out of Newcastle Central by Northumbrian pipes player Jack Armstrong, piper to the Duke of Northumberland. I thoroughly enjoyed this trip and found its sense of occasion quite impressive. Thousands of people turned out all the way from Newcastle to Woodburn to see the train. What impressed me more than anything, I think, was a group of railwaymen, with their memories, waving to us at Heaton sheds. Harold Williamson and the BBC TV news team were at Woodburn, and all BR regulations were sidestepped as we leapt down from the coaches at every available stop to get up to the locomotives, which are themselves to be withdrawn very shortly. What a turn-out, and what an occasion. The last day of 'The Wannie'.

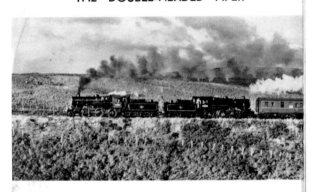

AN EYEMARK RAILWAYANA RELEASE

THE DOUBLE-HEADED PIPER

RECORDED HIGHLIGHTS OF THE COMMEMORATIVE FINAL STEAM TRAIN OVER THE WANSBECK VALLEY LINE—ROUTE OF THE FORMER NORTH BRITISH RAILWAY IN NORTHUMBERLAND.

The 'Wansbeck Piper' climbing Ray Fell en route to Woodburn, as depicted on the sleeve of the Eyemark recording *The Double-Headed Piper*.

Tuesday 20 December 1966
Observed a distant steam locomotive with wagons heading south along the Quarter-Mile this afternoon.

Friday 23 December 1966
This afternoon a steam locomotive ('K1'/'B1'?) headed north from Heaton Junction with a train of wagons.

Monday 23 January 1967
A wet day mostly. Bed at about 12.30am. I've just heard a steam engine clank through the Junction.

Thursday 2 February 1967
Watched a distant steam locomotive [not specified] making good ground northwards at about 10.00pm. And this coincided with a feature on BBC television news at 8.50 of the last BR steam locomotive to be repaired in England. It is 'Britannia' 'Pacific' No 70013 *Oliver Cromwell*.

Monday 3 April 1967
Saw a solitary 9F 2-10-0 with one brake van in Heaton Junction, by Chillingham Road bridge this morning.

Tuesday 2 May 1967
Noted a 'K1' (?) Class steam locomotive going north.

Tuesday 9 May 1967
Saw a BR Standard 2-6-0 heading north.

Wednesday 10 May 1967
A steam locomotive [unspecified] went north pulling a 'dead' one, a 'Q6' or 'J26'/'J27'. [Perhaps these were heading for Hughes Bolckow Shipbreakers at Blyth, just north of Newcastle, where at this time many steam locomotives met their end.]

The end of 'A4' No 60001 *Sir Ronald Matthews* at Hughes Bolckow shipbreakers, Blyth, Northumberland, 1964.

Tuesday 16 May 1967

Saw a steam locomotive (a 'J27'?) going north light engine.

Friday 21 July 1967

Momentous news in the *Evening Chronicle* is that 'A4' *Sir Nigel Gresley* is coming into Newcastle Central from Peterborough on Sunday. But the time is not stipulated. On no account must I miss it and I must endeavour to find out the time. The prospect of reliving an 'A4' 'experience' excites me as much as anything can, made even greater by memory. To some this would seem an absurd way of talking about a steam locomotive, but not for me with all my associations and the imaginative vigour that used to be set to work by steam, as recently as 1962 – now a distant prospect.

Sunday 23 July 1967

Phoned the Central station to ask about the times of the special train. Arrived there for 1.15pm. It was due in at 1.52pm but eventually arrived at 2.20pm I had a distant view of *Sir Nigel Gresley* at Gateshead MPD across the Tyne, as it was taking the curve onto the King Edward Bridge. There was no sign of steam as it hurried across the river and then moved more slowly along No 10 platform with two or three blasts on its chime whistle. It was painted in LNER Garter Blue with gold-lettered numbers 4498. Quite a crowd was there to see it. All told, it remained for about 3 minutes in the station, uncoupled and moved quickly away and onto the High Level Bridge heading towards Gateshead. I also saw Deltic D9001 *St Paddy* on a southbound passenger train and D9002 *King's Own Yorkshire Light Infantry* on the northbound 'Flying Scotsman'.

Saturday 16 December 1967

[Journeying from Birmingham on the 11.30am train to Newcastle I note:] ...saw a working steam locomotive at York, a Stanier Class 5 4-6-0.

Friday 19 January 1968

[As a postgraduate student, at what was then the new University of Warwick at Coventry, I transcribed into my diary a short piece from a feature in the *Coventry Evening Telegraph* on this day:] 'The magic of steam still captures the imagination of young and old, though I suppose many of you have not seen the great steam locomotives pulling express trains', adding my own comment, 'This is the final sadness, because it makes a pronouncement on me, too.'

Sunday 11 August 1968

At night I watched a television programme on *Flying Scotsman*'s journey of 1 May this year; 40th anniversary of the non-stop King's Cross-Edinburgh run, which was achieved again. The photography was first class, especially the sequence shot from a distance where *Flying Scotsman* comes onto the King Edward Bridge, Newcastle. The emotive music at that point, with all my memories, was almost too much; especially as I was watching this programme on the day of the very last scheduled steam train to run for British Railways.

✳

Here the story ends. It can be seen, from the barely concealed emotion of the last entry, how inadequately this little artless social history expresses my true feelings for a vanished era. All that remains to say is that I'm grateful to have been born in time to have caught the end of it and, in a very minor way, been enabled to preserve in these pages some of my memories of those epic days.

> Whither is fled the visionary gleam?
> Where is it now, the glory and the steam?

COMING SOON...

The next volume in the series

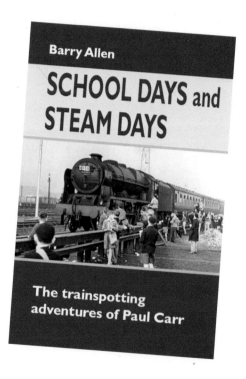

Barry Allen

SCHOOL DAYS and STEAM DAYS

The trainspotting adventures of Paul Carr

Due Spring 2012
Hardback   160pp   Illustrated   RRP: £10.00
ISBN: 978 1 85794 395 5